low fat

100 BEST RECIPES

LINDA DOESER

This is a Parragon Book
This edition published in 2004

Parragon
Queen Street House
4 Queen Street
Bath BA1 1HE
United Kingdom

Created and produced by
The Bridgewater Book Company Ltd,
Lewes, East Sussex

Photographer Ian Parsons

ISBN: 0–75259–932–1

Printed in Malaysia

NOTE

This book uses metric and imperial measurements. Follow the same
units of measurement throughout; do not mix metric and imperial. All spoon
measurements are level: teaspoons are assumed to be 5 ml and tablespoons are
assumed to be 15 ml. Unless otherwise stated, milk is assumed to be full fat,
eggs and individual vegetables such as potatoes are medium, and pepper is
freshly ground black pepper.

The times given for each recipe are an approximate guide only.
The preparation times may differ according to the techniques used by different
people and the cooking times may vary as a result of the type of oven used.
Ovens should be preheated to the specified temperature. If using a fan-assisted
oven, check the manufacturer's instructions for adjusting the time and temperature.
The preparation times include chilling and marinating times, where appropriate.

The nutritional information provided for each recipe is per serving or per
portion. Optional ingredients, variations or serving suggestions have not been
included in the calculations.

Recipes using raw or very lightly cooked eggs should be avoided
by infants, the elderly, pregnant women, convalescents and anyone
suffering from an illness.

contents

introduction

As we are becoming more aware of how we can improve our own and our families' health, low-fat cooking is becoming increasingly popular. However, low-fat food is often wrongly perceived as being 'diet' food and, therefore, boring, bland and unappetizing. This is simply not true and this book will help to change any misconceptions. Low-fat cooking is healthier and often less expensive, and there is a huge variety of tasty dishes.

From day-to-day family suppers to sophisticated dinner parties, this book is packed with delicious recipe ideas and tips. You will find many family favourites in the following pages, such as Easy Gazpacho (see page 20), Pasta with Low-fat Pesto (see page 44), Meatballs with Tomato Relish (see page 84) and Smoked Haddock Pie (see page 124). There is even a selection of low-fat sandwich fillings for quick and easy snacks.

While nutritionists and health professionals agree that most people in the Western world eat too much fat, this does not mean that you should try to cut it out of your diet completely. Everybody needs to consume a certain amount of fat for general health and wellbeing. Fats are a concentrated source of energy and provide valuable vitamins. Essential fats are – as their name suggests – essential. The type of fat consumed is as important as the quantity (see page 6). However, as a rule, your daily intake of fats should not exceed more than 30 per cent of the day's total average of 2,000 calories (for adults). As each gram of fat provides nine calories, simple arithmetic shows that the average daily intake of fat should be no more than 66.7 g (2½ oz).

Some people can eat nothing but burgers and fries and still stay slim, but this does not mean that they are healthy. By doing more exercise and having a higher metabolic rate, you can burn off more of the fat you have consumed, but you will not be so healthy as your friend who consumes less fat and exercises moderately. Whether you want to lose weight, have been told to eat less fat by your doctor or simply want to improve your family's health, use this book to guide you to a healthier and happier lifestyle. This book also includes tips on how to choose lower-fat ingredients in place of the butter, cream, cheese and red meats to which we have all become accustomed, as well as advice on healthy cooking techniques and useful equipment.

changing your eating patterns

Food is always more appetising if it is presented attractively. All of the recipes in this book use colour and style, as well as flavour and texture, to make your meal thoroughly enjoyable. If you are entertaining guests, why not try one of the following combinations? For vegetarian guests, serve Lentil & Tomato Soup (see page 17), followed by Roast Summer Vegetables (see page 56) and Lemon Granita (see page 163). Serve Parma Ham with Figs (see page 35), Beef in Beer (see page 85) and Hot Chocolate Cherries (see page 154) as a winter meal for meat-lovers. Chicken & Asparagus Timbales (see page 30), followed by Lamb Tagine (see page 94) and Peach Sorbet (see page 164), is an ideal meal for a dinner party.

The recipes featured in this book are just a few of the many delicious low-fat meals you can make. They vary in difficulty from quick and easy to more time-consuming and skilful. Many of the dishes are also suitable for freezing and re-heating in an oven or microwave. You can even take them to work and heat them up at lunchtime, leaving no excuses for indulging in takeaways.

types of fat

Keeping track of which fats to eat and which to avoid, counting calories and keeping a wary eye on sugar and salt content can all seem overwhelming. The thing to remember is that too many saturated fats are harmful, but unsaturated fats in moderation are beneficial.

You will find saturated fats in foods such as red meat, butter, hard cheese (like Cheddar), biscuits, cakes, pastries and chocolate. Although they are mostly found in animal products, there are some vegetable sources too. Coconut and palm oil are both high in saturated fats, as are most fats that are solid at room temperature.

There are two different types of unsaturated fats – monounsaturated and polyunsaturated. Monounsaturated fats are better for you than saturated fats, but are not so good as polyunsaturated fats. Monounsaturated fats are found in olive oil, rapeseed oil, nuts, seeds, oily fish and avocados. These are fine if consumed in moderate quantities and are thought to reduce cholesterol level in the blood. This may explain why there is a low incidence of heart disease in some Mediterranean countries where olive oil, avocados and oily fish are eaten regularly.

The body needs polyunsaturated fats for various functions. Both omega-3 and omega-6 fatty acids are classed by nutritionists as essential. Omega-3 fatty acids are needed for healthy cells and brain development. Polyunsaturated fats help to protect against heart disease, arthritis and some other medical conditions. Polyunsaturated fats are found in fish oils, oily fish, walnuts, olive oil and sunflower oil. They are usually liquid at room temperature.

Be careful of processed oils labelled 'hydrogenated vegetable oils', as some of the good unsaturated fats are converted to unhealthy saturated fats – or trans fats – by the process used to make them.

cholesterol

Raised cholesterol levels in the blood are regarded as a cause for concern, as levels that are constantly high or rising are thought to cause heart disease. The best way to avoid this happening is to eat a varied and balanced diet. Cut out, or at least cut down on, foods such as solid cooking fats (lard and hard margarine), biscuits, cakes, pastries, chocolate, fatty meat, processed foods (including sausages), and full-fat dairy products (butter, cream and hard cheeses). Medical research shows that if you cut down to almost no saturated fats, you may be able to reduce your blood cholesterol level by more than 10 per cent. Foods thought to be helpful in reducing blood cholesterol levels include wholemeal bread, Granary bread, cereal containing cooked bran, rolled oats, oranges, apples, bananas, figs, prunes, sweetcorn, garlic, onions, red kidney beans and other pulses. Try having Fruity Flapjacks (see page 173) as a low-cholesterol alternative to cakes.

a balanced diet

There are five main food groups, and you should try to eat a certain amount from each group daily. The first group consists of fruit and vegetables (not potatoes), and provides you mainly with vitamins and minerals. The advice is to eat at least five portions from this group per day and that at least some of them should be uncooked. This may sound like a lot, but you will be able to eat the daily recommendation if you spread it throughout the day – for example, choose a banana and cereal for breakfast, a sandwich with salad for lunch and steamed chicken with broccoli, carrots and peas for dinner. Try to snack on healthy alternatives to crisps and chocolate, such as fruit.

The second group includes staples such as rice, pasta, bread, potatoes and cereals. These contain complex carbohydrates, which release energy at a steady rate, and dietary fibre, which aids digestion. It is recommended that we try to consume several servings of these foods each day. Having a rice salad (with a low-fat dressing) for lunch, potatoes with dinner and Fat-free Marble Cake (see page 168) for dessert will be an adequate intake for most people. This group helps to keep your digestive system working efficiently and is thought to help reduce the chances of stomach and bowel cancers.

The third food group is the protein foods – meat, fish and poultry. Red meat can be high in saturated fats and you need to trim off any visible fat before cooking. Poultry and fish are the healthiest ingredients. Eat plenty of oily fish, such as sardines, mackerel, tuna, salmon and herrings, as they are rich in omega-3 essential fatty acids. You do not need to eat foods from this group every day if you have a mixed diet. When you do eat them, you need only small quantities. About 25 per cent of the fat we consume comes from meat and meat products. Even trimmed meats, such as lamb chops, pork loin and fillet steak, can contain high amounts of fats. Vegetarians can sometimes have an inadequate intake of protein. They should take care to eat a varied diet that includes tofu and other vegetable proteins.

The fourth food group is made up of dairy products, including milk, cheese and cream. You need a moderate amount of these foods daily. Growing children, pregnant women and the elderly, especially those suffering from a bone disease such as osteoporosis, require a higher intake of calcium and should adjust their diets accordingly. Most dairy products contain a very high proportion of fats, and eating large amounts can make it more difficult to lose weight or keep blood cholesterol levels down. About 20 per cent of the fat we consume comes from this food group.

Be careful about the fifth food group. It consists of foods that contain fat and sugar, such as margarine, chocolate and sweet pastries. You need only very small amounts of food from this group as you will obtain the small intake of fat you require from other food groups.

Being aware of hidden fats is important. It is easy to cut down on fatty foods, but knowing where to look for the real low-fat alternatives is essential. Many nuts and seeds are rich in essential fatty acids, but also have quite a high overall fat content. Even trimmed 'lean' meat can contain up to 10 per cent fat.

A varied diet is a healthy diet, and you should aim to eat different foods each day, as they all have different combinations and quantities of nutrients. Try different types of pasta, such as Fettuccine with Smoked Salmon (see page 46) and Rigatoni with Squid (see page 142). When cooking pasta, resist the temptation to add a few drops of oil to the saucepan to prevent it sticking, as this raises the fat content. Making use of exotic fruits and vegetables will also make a low-fat diet more interesting.

low-fat cooking techniques

You may be used to putting a knob of butter or lard into the frying pan before adding the streaky bacon – this doesn't mean that you should. Instead of adding the saturated fat, try grilling without any added fat. Instead of streaky, try lean bacon and trim off any visible fat. You could even get rid of the bacon altogether. Knowing what the alternatives are is the key to enjoying your new low-fat diet. You don't have to forego everything you enjoy eating. Sitting down to a family meal together can be one of the most pleasurable parts of your day.

It is worthwhile investing in good-quality, non-stick cookware. Cast iron, stainless steel and heavy-gauge aluminium are ideal and you will find that you need very little fat, as the heat is evenly distributed. If you need to add fat, use oils high in unsaturated fats, such as olive or sunflower oil. Cans of 'spray oils' are even more effective at minimising the amount you use, as you can give the saucepan a light, even coat.

As a rule, avoid frying, as it is the least healthy way of cooking. Stir-frying is better as long as you use very little oil. Use a good-quality wok and keep the temperature high, tossing the ingredients constantly so that they do not stick. Try Prawn Stir-fry (see page 144). The best advice about deep-frying is: don't!

Vegetables can be cooked in many ways and are often especially healthy when eaten raw. Try cooking them in juice, stock and/or wine for a tasty alternative to oil. Steamed vegetables have a more vibrant colour, firmer texture and retain more nutrients than boiled vegetables. Boiling vegetables is a no-fat way of cooking, but it also destroys many of their nutrients, especially vitamins. Try microwaving as a quick alternative to boiling or steaming.

Grilling is one of the healthiest methods of cooking and a number of foods can be cooked this way. Thread diced chicken and vegetables onto skewers, then barbecue or grill as kebabs. Barbecuing imparts a beautiful flavour to the food and is healthy, although be careful to eat vegetables to balance the protein. Try not to burn barbecue food, as this is not only unappetizing, but is also believed to be carcinogenic (cancer-causing).

Griddling in a ridged griddle pan is a healthy compromise between shallow-frying and grilling. The food cooks rapidly and if oil is needed, lightly brushing over the griddle pan is all that is required. If poached chicken seems like boiled meat to you, try poaching chicken breasts in stock with white wine and herbs. You do not need to use any oil and can steam vegetables over the saucepan while the meat is cooking. Poaching is also ideal for fish.

Instead of adding flavourings as you cook, you can use a marinade. Meat and poultry are made tender by marinating overnight or for at least 4 hours in a mixture of lemon juice, oil, herbs, garlic and either vinegar or alcohol. Do not marinate fish for longer than 1 hour.

When you are baking desserts, use good-quality bakeware. Use greaseproof paper or baking paper to eliminate the need to coat the cake tins in butter before adding the mixture. A light brushing of oil is sufficient.

from high fat to low fat

When buying meat, ask your butcher to trim off any visible fat or to remove the bone so that you can easily trim the meat. If you shop in a supermarket, it is not easy to see what you are buying if it is pre-packed. Buy from the delicatessen or butcher and do not be afraid to ask him to put a piece back and get you another.

Many supermarkets now stock an extensive range of low-fat and low-calorie products, such as milk, cheese, yogurt, salad dressings, crisps and biscuits. However, even if the label says 'low fat', it is still best to have a look at the ingredients list. Avoid products labelled 'reduced fat', as they may have a very high saturated fat content.

Low-fat spreads are available in every shop and supermarket and it can be confusing to read all the labels, which make various claims. Generally, some are only for spreading and others are only for cooking. Olive oil provides the best flavour when cooking, but can be expensive to use regularly. For spreading, you can buy the very low-fat spreads, but these have a high water content and are not suitable for cooking. Spreads labelled low-fat or half-fat are suitable for spreading and baking and have a fat content of about 40 per cent, compared with the very low-fat spreads with about 20 per cent.

Gradually changing and enhancing your diet is far better and safer than suddenly stopping eating one thing and switching to another. There are many ways to re-adjust your diet and that of your family without extra financial cost or effort in the kitchen.

To begin with, eat less of the foods that contain lots of saturated fats. Buy low-fat spreads and olive oil or polyunsaturated oils for cooking.

Limit fatty meats, such as lamb and pork, to occasional treats and eat chicken, turkey, fish and venison instead. Trim any visible fat from the meat and remove the skin. If you are fond of a roast dinner, try putting a chicken on a rack with a roasting tin underneath. Cover it with herbs and garlic and baste occasionally with stock – cook at the same temperature and for the same length of time as a normal roast. Instead of making gravy the traditional way, try reducing stock or vegetable cooking water and freezing it in meal-size portions, then thicken with cornflour and add salt, pepper and herbs.

Instead of basing meals around meat, try a meal based around eggs, such as Mexican Eggs (see page 58), or around vegetables, such as Layered Vegetable Bake (see page 64). Sausages can be high in saturated fats – choose low-fat varieties or make your own. Prick them with a fork so that the fat can run out, place on a rack and grill.

Even if you are not a vegetarian, use tofu in place of meat sometimes for a healthy, low-fat alternative. Try Vegetable & Tofu Stir-fry (see page 110).

Full-fat dairy products can raise blood cholesterol levels and contribute to obesity. This is a high risk for vegetarians, who often rely too heavily on cheese for protein. Avoid these full-fat products altogether and switch to semi-skimmed or skimmed milk products, which will make a huge difference to your fat intake.

Low-fat yogurts are readily available in almost all food shops and are a great idea for a healthy lunch. Buy low-fat natural yogurt and use it as a substitute for cream to thicken sauces and add to desserts. A bowl of low-fat natural yogurt with honey or jam (which contain no fat at all) makes a healthy and delicious start to the day. Low-fat and no-fat fromage frais are also healthy options which can be used in both sweet and savoury dishes.

Instead of buying French fries and crisps, look for low-fat crackers, breadsticks and savoury biscuits. If you cannot find any, you can make your own by baking thin slices of potato coated with herbs and spices. Most supermarkets now have a range of very low-fat crisps, most of them baked with little or no oil. If you eat out and find that everything is served with chips, ask if they have baked potatoes, rice or pasta.

Avoid eating cakes, biscuits, chocolate, tortilla chips and pastries and resist vending machines and canteens at work. If you find a health food shop too inconvenient, make your own snacks. Fresh fruit and vegetables are the best things to snack on. Dried fruits, such as apricots, figs, prunes and raisins, are also a healthier option, although high in sugar. Try slices of carrot, pieces of cauliflower, spring onion, radishes, cucumber or hard-boiled eggs with a dip, such as low-fat hummus, natural yogurt with herbs or ready-made low-fat dips.

Slices of apple dipped in honey can be a delicious quick snack if you have a sweet tooth. Sorbets, such as Peach Sorbet (see page 164), make a good low-fat alternative to ice cream and are just as delicious on a hot summer's day. You can make muesli bars using rolled oats, and bran muffins and biscuits using low-fat ingredients. Instead of chocolate toppings, try making a yogurt topping. Canned fruit is also a good option, although you should avoid fruits that are preserved in syrup. Although there is no fat in syrup, the sugar content is high and natural fruit juice is better.

If you regularly eat takeaways, this is one of the first things to address. Almost everything seems to be deep-fried in saturated fats and is bad for your cholesterol levels, your weight and your heart. Try home-made burgers and you will discover a new taste experience, as well as cutting down your fat intake. Takeaway pizza is high in saturated fats and the best thing you can do is make your own at home. If you do end up getting a takeaway pizza, blot each slice well with kitchen paper to soak up excess fat on the surface. You can adapt all sorts of traditional and favourite meals to a low-fat diet, just as you can adapt them for a diabetic, vegetarian or low-sodium diet.

the low-fat family

Exercise is as important as eating healthily and nobody really has any excuse for not doing some exercise. Walking is one of the best ways to burn off extra fat and calories, and aids digestion. Moderate exercise a little while after a meal is safe, but you shouldn't begin a heavy workout soon after eating or you will give yourself indigestion. If you are trying to involve your whole family in a lifestyle change, go for walks together after a low-fat lunch. A picnic is the ideal setting for a low-fat meal and many recipes in this book are easy to make, pack up and carry. Ideas for picnic nibbles include Trout Mousse (see page 38) with low-fat crackers or breadsticks, or Crudités with Garlic Chive & Coriander Dip (see page 28). Persuading the family to eat a low-fat diet with you can be difficult. If part of your aim is to lose weight, point out all the benefits to your family.

Be careful about putting children on diets. If your child is overweight, consult your doctor before making any drastic changes in their diet. Children need different amounts of nutrients and are very sensitive to changes in lifestyle. Cutting down on crisps, chocolate, sweets, fast food and fatty snacks is the first step and this can be done without seeing a doctor first. Children under five years old should not be given skimmed or semi-skimmed milk or dairy products made from them.

Children will invariably complain about eating vegetables, but if you serve them in an attractive way, perhaps with a dressing, you are more likely to get a positive response. Snacks for children could include breadsticks and dips, home-made crisps, fruit slices, and fruit kebabs dipped in honey and grilled (on skewers without sharp points), and home-made low-fat ice cream. Many of these things are a good idea for healthy packed lunches to take to school. Try Scrumptious Sandwiches (see page 48), Vegetable Samosas (see page 62) and Spicy Chicken with Naan (see page 50) – with a little less spice for very young ones.

Many people are very wary of low-fat 'diets', yet they often pay little attention to how their evening meal is prepared. If your family is used to steak, egg and chips smothered in ketchup, serve grilled steak with the fat trimmed off, baked potato with low-fat spread, steamed vegetables or salad and home-made low-fat mayonnaise or tomato chutney. You do not need to tell them that the meal is low-fat – simply serve it up and wait for their requests for a second helping!

basic recipes

vegetable stock

makes: 2 litres/3½ pints
preparation time: 10 minutes
cooking time: 40 minutes

2 tbsp sunflower oil
115 g/4 oz onions, finely chopped
115 g/4 oz leeks, finely chopped
115 g/4 oz carrots, finely chopped
4 celery sticks, finely chopped
85 g/3 oz fennel, finely chopped
85 g/3 oz tomatoes, finely chopped
2.25 litres/4 pints water
1 bouquet garni

1 Heat the oil in a large saucepan. Add the onions and leeks and cook over a low heat, stirring occasionally, for 5 minutes, or until softened.

2 Add the remaining vegetables, cover and cook over a low heat, stirring occasionally, for 10 minutes. Add the water and bouquet garni, bring to the boil and simmer for 20 minutes.

3 Sieve, cool and store in the refrigerator. Use immediately or freeze in portions for up to 3 months.

cook's tip

To make the bouquet garni, tie 4 fresh parsley stems, 1 clove, 1 bay leaf and 4 peppercorns in a piece of clean muslin.

fish stock

makes: 1.3 litres/2¼ pints
preparation time: 10 minutes
cooking time: 30 minutes

650 g/1 lb 7 oz white fish heads, bones and trimmings, rinsed
1 onion, sliced
2 celery sticks, chopped
1 carrot, sliced
1 bay leaf
4 fresh parsley sprigs
4 black peppercorns
½ lemon, sliced

1.3 litres/2¼ pints water
125 ml/4 fl oz dry white wine

1 Place the fish heads, bones and trimmings in a large saucepan. Add the remaining ingredients, then bring to the boil and skim off the foam that rises to the surface with a slotted spoon.

2 Reduce the heat, partially cover and simmer gently for 25 minutes.

3 Sieve the stock, without pressing down on the contents of the sieve. Cool and store in the refrigerator. Use immediately or freeze in portions for up to 3 months.

variation

Shellfish stock has a beautifully delicate flavour. Use prawn heads and shells with white fish trimmings.

chicken stock

makes: 2.5 litres/4½ pints
preparation time: 15 minutes, plus 30 minutes chilling
cooking time: 3½ hours

1.3 kg/3 lb chicken wings and necks
2 onions, cut into wedges
4 litres/7 pints water
2 carrots, roughly chopped
2 celery sticks, roughly chopped
10 fresh parsley sprigs
4 fresh thyme sprigs
2 bay leaves
10 black peppercorns

1 Put the chicken wings and necks and the onions in a large, heavy-based saucepan and cook over a low heat, stirring frequently, until lightly browned all over.

2 Add the water and stir to scrape off sediment on the base of the pan. Bring to the boil and skim off any foam. Add the remaining ingredients, partially cover and simmer gently for 3 hours.

3 Sieve, cool and chill in the refrigerator. When cold, carefully remove and discard the layer of fat that has set on the surface. Use immediately or freeze in portions for up to 6 months.

beef stock

makes: 1.7 litres/3 pints
preparation time: 15 minutes, plus 30 minutes chilling
cooking time: 4¼ hours

1 kg/2 lb 4 oz beef marrow bones, sawn into 7.5-cm/3-inch pieces
650 g/1 lb 7 oz stewing beef in 1 piece
2.8 litres/5 pints water
4 cloves
2 onions, halved
2 celery sticks, roughly chopped
8 peppercorns
1 bouquet garni

1 Place the bones in the base of a large, heavy-based saucepan and put the beef on top. Add the water and bring to the boil over a low heat, skimming off all the foam that rises to the surface.

2 Press a clove into each onion half and add to the pan with the celery, peppercorns and bouquet garni. Reduce the heat, partially cover and simmer very gently for 3 hours. Remove the meat and simmer for a further 1 hour.

3 Sieve, cool and chill in the refrigerator. When cold, carefully remove and discard the layer of fat that has set on the surface. Use immediately or freeze in portions for up to 6 months.

low-fat mayonnaise

makes: 200 ml/7 fl oz
preparation time: 10 minutes,
plus 10 minutes standing
cooking time: 0 minutes

4 hard-boiled egg yolks
2 tbsp white wine vinegar
2 tbsp lemon juice
1 tsp Dijon mustard
salt and pepper
4 tbsp low-fat natural yogurt

1 Mix the egg yolks, vinegar, lemon juice and mustard together, then season to taste with salt and pepper. Mash thoroughly with a fork to blend.

2 Beat in the yogurt, 1 tablespoon at a time, until incorporated.

3 Cover with clingfilm and leave to stand for 10 minutes to allow the flavours to mingle.

saffron sauce

serves: 6
preparation time: 15 minutes
cooking time: 0 minutes

1 egg yolk
pinch of salt
pinch of powdered saffron
¼ tsp ground coriander
¼ tsp ground cumin
150 ml/5 fl oz sunflower oil
1½ tsp white wine vinegar
1½ tsp lemon juice
150 ml/5 fl oz low-fat natural yogurt

1 Put the egg yolk in a bowl and beat with the salt, then stir in the saffron, coriander and cumin.

2 Add the sunflower oil, one drop at a time, beating constantly. When half the oil has been incorporated, add the remainder in a steady stream, beating constantly.

3 Stir in the vinegar and lemon juice and fold in the yogurt. Cover and chill in the refrigerator until required.

cook's tip

For a quick and easy low-fat dressing, put 1 tablespoon of clear honey in a bowl, add 6 tablespoons of low-fat natural yogurt and beat until blended. Season to taste.

Fat content of common foods

The following figures show the weight of fat in grams per 100 g/3½ oz of each food.

vegetables

Aubergine	0.4 g
Beetroot, raw	0.1 g
Broccoli	0.9 g
Cabbage	0.4 g
Carrots	0.3 g
Cauliflower	0.9 g
Celery	0.2 g
Chips, home-made	6.7 g
Chips, oven	4.2 g
Chips, ready-made	12.4 g
Courgettes	0.4 g
Cucumber	0.1 g
Mushrooms	0.5 g
Onions	0.2 g
Peas	1.5 g
Potatoes	0.2 g
Tomatoes	0.3 g

pulses

Black-eyed beans, cooked	1.8 g
Butter beans, canned	0.5 g
Chickpeas, canned	2.9 g
Hummus	12.6 g
Red kidney beans, canned	0.6 g
Red lentils, cooked	0.4 g

fish and shellfish

Cod fillets, raw	0.7 g
Crab, canned	0.5 g
Crab, cooked	2.0 g
Haddock, raw	0.6 g
Lemon sole, raw	1.5 g
Mussels	2.0 g
Prawns	0.9 g
Trout, grilled	5.4 g
Tuna, canned in brine	0.6 g
Tuna, canned in oil	9.0 g

meat

Bacon, streaky	39.5 g
Beef, minced, raw	16.2 g
Beef, minced, extra lean, raw	9.6 g
Rump steak, trimmed, raw	4.1 g
Lamb, trimmed, raw	8.3 g
Pork, trimmed, raw	4.0 g
Chicken breast portion, raw	1.1 g
Chicken, roasted	12.5 g
Duck, meat only, raw	6.5 g
Duck, roasted	38.1 g
Turkey, meat only, raw	1.6 g

dairy and fats

Brie	26.9 g
Butter	81.7 g
Cheddar	34.4 g
Cheddar, reduced-fat	15.0 g
Cream cheese	47.4 g
Cream, double	48.0 g
Cream, double, reduced-fat	24.0 g
Cream, single	19.1 g
Cream, whipping	39.3 g
Crème fraîche	40.0 g
Crème fraîche, reduced-fat	15.0 g
Edam	25.4 g
Feta	20.2 g
Fromage frais	7.1 g
Fromage frais, very low-fat	0.2 g
Lard	99.0 g
Low-fat spread	40.5 g
Low-fat spread, very	25.0 g
Margarine	81.6 g
Milk, full-fat	3.9 g
Milk, skimmed	0.1 g
Parmesan	32.7 g
Skimmed milk soft cheese	trace
Yogurt, low-fat	0.8 g
Yogurt, Greek	9.1 g
Yogurt, reduced-fat, Greek	5.0 g

oils

Corn oil	99.9 g
Olive oil	99.9 g
Safflower oil	99.9 g

eggs

Whole egg	10.8 g
Egg yolk	30.5 g
Egg white	trace

dressings

Fat-free dressing	1.2 g
Mayonnaise	75.6 g
Mayonnaise, reduced calorie	28.1 g
Vinaigrette	49.4 g

cereals and baking

Bread, brown	2.0 g
Bread, white	1.9 g
Bread, wholemeal	2.5 g
Chocolate, milk	30.7 g
Chocolate, plain	28.0 g
Cornflakes	0.7 g
Croissants	20.3 g
Digestive biscuits	20.9 g
Digestive biscuits, reduced-fat	16.4 g
Doughnut, jam	14.5 g
Sponge cake, fat-free	6.1 g
Flapjack	26.6 g
Flour, white	1.3 g
Flour, wholemeal	2.2 g
Madeira cake	16.9 g
Muesli	5.9 g
Naan bread	12.5 g
Pasta, white, uncooked	1.8 g
Pasta, wholemeal, uncooked	2.5 g
Pitta bread	1.2 g
Rice, brown, uncooked	2.8 g
Rice, white, uncooked	3.6 g
Shortbread	26.1 g
Sugar, white	0.3 g
Sultana bran	1.6 g

preserves

Honey	0 g
Jam	0.26 g
Lemon curd	5.0 g

processed foods

Baked beans in tomato sauce	0.6 g
Burger, grilled	14.0 g
Burger, fried	17.0 g
Fish fingers	12.0 g
Pork pie	27.0 g
Salami	45.2 g
Sausages	22.0 g
Sausages, low-fat	6.0 g
Sausage roll	36.4 g

fruit

Apples, eating	0.1 g
Apricots	0.1 g
Avocados	19.5 g
Bananas	0.3 g
Cherries	0.1 g
Currants, black/red/white	1.0 g
Dried mixed fruit	0.4 g
Grapefruit	0.1 g
Olives, in brine	11.0 g
Oranges	0.1 g
Peaches	0.1 g
Pears	0.1 g
Prunes	0.2 g

nuts

Almonds	55.8 g
Brazil nuts	68.2 g
Hazelnuts	63.5 g
Peanuts, plain	46.1 g
Peanut butter	53.7 g
Pine kernels	68.6 g
Walnuts	68.5 g

soups & appetizers

Few things are simpler and more delicious than home-made soup. The recipes here range from winter warmers for family suppers to chilled summer soup, as well as delicately flavoured elegant soups to grace a dinner party table. The secret of success lies in using a well-made, flavoursome stock. An added advantage of home-made stock (see page 11) is that you have total control over what goes into it and you can be sure to skim off every last trace of fat from the surface once it has been chilled. You can, of course, use stock cubes or bouillon powder, but do read the labels carefully before buying and try to find a brand that is not too salty.

The starters featured in this chapter include a mouthwatering selection of vegetarian specialities, as well as delicious dishes with fish, shellfish, chicken and Parma ham – and most of them with fewer than 10 g (¼ oz) of fat per serving. Some require no cooking at all and can be assembled in moments, while others are more elaborate and extravagant dishes for special occasions. There are tempting treats for every time of year, from wonderful ways with summery asparagus (see pages 30 and 34) to the spectacular Oysters Rockefeller (see page 41) for when there's an 'r' in the month, as well as any-time dishes, from easy Antipasto Mushrooms (see page 25) to sophisticated Trout Mousse (see page 38).

parisian pea soup

This is one occasion when cooking with just a little amount of butter is worthwhile because of its rather rich flavour.

INGREDIENTS

25 g/1 oz butter

2 shallots, finely chopped

450 g/1 lb shelled peas

2 Little Gem or 1 small cos or

Webbs lettuce, shredded

1.2 litres/2 pints Vegetable Stock

(see page 11)

pinch of freshly grated nutmeg

salt and pepper

2–3 tbsp low-fat soured cream

(optional)

fresh chives, to garnish

NUTRITIONAL INFORMATION

Calories	148
Protein	8g
Carbohydrate	14g
Sugars	4g
Fat	7g
Saturates	4g

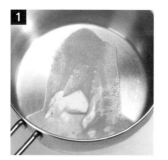

cook's tip

Using home-made Chicken Stock (see page 11) instead of the Vegetable Stock gives this delicate soup a fuller flavour, but also increases the amount of fat slightly.

1 Melt the butter in a large, heavy-based saucepan. Add the shallots and cook over a medium heat, stirring occasionally, for 5 minutes, or until softened.

2 Add the peas, shredded lettuce and stock to the saucepan and season to taste with nutmeg, salt and pepper. Bring to the boil, then reduce the heat, cover and simmer for 10–15 minutes, or until the peas are tender.

3 Remove the saucepan from the heat and leave to cool slightly. Transfer the mixture to a blender or food processor and process until a smooth purée forms. Return the soup to the rinsed-out saucepan and heat through gently until hot. Ladle the soup into 4 large, warmed serving bowls. Top with a spoonful of soured cream, if using, garnish with a few fresh chives and serve.

lentil & tomato soup

⏱ **cook: 50 mins**   ⏱ **prep: 20 mins**   **serves 4**

This fresh-tasting and colourful soup is substantial enough to serve on its own with some crusty fresh bread for a light lunch or supper.

NUTRITIONAL INFORMATION	
Calories	158
Protein	. . . . .9g
Carbohydrate	. . . . .24g
Sugars	. . . . 6g
Fat	. . . . .4g
Saturates	. . . . .1g

INGREDIENTS

1 tbsp corn or sunflower oil

1 onion, finely chopped

1 garlic glove, crushed

½ tsp ground cumin

½ tsp ground coriander

450 g/1 lb tomatoes, peeled, deseeded and chopped

125 g/4½ oz split red lentils

1.2 litres/2 pints Vegetable Stock (see page 11)

salt and pepper

finely chopped fresh coriander, to garnish

(see page 11)

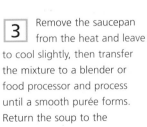

1   Heat the oil in a large saucepan. Add the onion and cook over a low heat, stirring occasionally, for 5 minutes, or until softened.

2   Stir in the garlic, cumin, ground coriander, tomatoes and lentils and cook, stirring constantly, for a further 4 minutes. Pour in the stock, bring to the boil, then reduce the heat and simmer gently for 30–40 minutes, or until the lentils are tender. Season to taste with salt and pepper.

3   Remove the saucepan from the heat and leave to cool slightly, then transfer the mixture to a blender or food processor and process until a smooth purée forms. Return the soup to the rinsed-out saucepan and re-heat gently until hot. Ladle the soup into 4 large, warmed soup bowls, garnish with chopped fresh coriander and serve immediately.

cook's tip

Always season lentils with salt after they have been cooked, otherwise they will become tough and may spoil the finished dish.

chinese noodle soup

serves 4   **prep: 10 mins**   **cook: 15 mins**

This soup has everything going for it – not only is it extremely low in fat, but it takes little time to make, looks intriguing and is a mouthwatering combination of flavours and textures.

INGREDIENTS

1.2 litres/2 pints Vegetable Stock
(see page 11)
2 tbsp light soy sauce
1½ tsp saffron threads
4 spring onions
2 courgettes
2 large tomatoes
1 garlic clove
115 g/4 oz rice noodles
pepper
finely snipped fresh garlic chives,
to garnish

NUTRITIONAL INFORMATION

Calories 135

Protein 3g

Carbohydrate 29g

Sugars 3g

Fat 1g

Saturates 0g

variation

To give the soup a spicy lift, season with 1–2 pinches of cayenne pepper instead of the ground black pepper.

1 Pour the vegetable stock into a large, heavy-based saucepan, add the light soy sauce, then bring the mixture to the boil over a medium heat.

2 Put the saffron threads into a mortar and lightly crush with a pestle, then stir the crushed saffron threads into the hot stock.

3 Prepare the vegetables. Slice the spring onions into rings, then cut the courgettes into batons and peel and chop the tomatoes. Chop the garlic finely, then add all the vegetables to the stock with the rice noodles. Bring the soup back to the boil over a medium heat, then cover and simmer for 5 minutes.

4 Season the soup to taste with pepper and ladle into 4 warmed serving bowls. Garnish with finely snipped garlic chives and serve immediately.

spicy vegetable soup

cook: 15 mins   **prep: 5 mins**   **serves 4**

Wake up the taste buds with a hint of curry spices in this easy-to-prepare vegetable soup. Served as a light lunch with Indian bread, such as chapati or paratha, it is a healthy option.

NUTRITIONAL INFORMATION

Calories 75

Protein 3g

Carbohydrate 8g

Sugars 5g

Fat 4g

Saturates 1g

INGREDIENTS

1 tbsp sunflower or corn oil

280 g/10 oz leeks, thinly sliced

2 garlic cloves, finely chopped

½ tsp grated fresh root ginger

½ tsp ground cumin

½ tsp ground coriander

½ tsp ground turmeric

1.2 litres/2 pints Vegetable Stock

(see page 11)

450 g/1 lb tomatoes, finely diced

2 courgettes, cut into batons

salt and pepper

3 tbsp chopped fresh coriander, to garnish

1   Heat the oil in a large, heavy-based saucepan. Add the sliced leeks, chopped garlic and ginger and cook over a medium heat, stirring occasionally, for 2 minutes. Stir in the cumin, ground coriander and turmeric and cook, stirring constantly, for 30 seconds.

2   Pour in the vegetable stock and stir well, then bring the mixture to the boil. Reduce the heat, cover and simmer for 5 minutes, then stir in the diced tomatoes and courgette batons. Cover and simmer for a further 3 minutes.

3   Season the soup to taste with salt and pepper, then ladle into 4 warmed serving bowls. Garnish with the chopped fresh coriander and serve.

variation

For a more subtle flavour to this soup, substitute ½ teaspoon crushed saffron threads for the ground turmeric.

easy gazpacho

serves 4 **prep: 10 mins, plus 2 hrs chilling** **cook: 0 mins**

The perfect choice for alfresco dining, this classic chilled soup is packed with fresh flavours. As no cooking is involved, the vegetables retain their colour and their valuable vitamins, and you remain cool in the kitchen.

INGREDIENTS

1 small cucumber, peeled and chopped

2 red peppers, deseeded and chopped

2 green peppers, deseeded and chopped

2 garlic cloves, roughly chopped

1 fresh basil sprig

600 ml/1 pint passata

1 tbsp extra virgin olive oil

1 tbsp red wine vinegar

1 tbsp balsamic vinegar

300 ml/10 fl oz Vegetable Stock (see page 11)

2 tbsp lemon juice

salt and pepper

TO SERVE

2 tbsp diced, peeled cucumber

2 tbsp finely chopped red onion

2 tbsp finely chopped red pepper

2 tbsp finely chopped green pepper

ice cubes

4 fresh basil sprigs

fresh crusty bread

NUTRITIONAL INFORMATION

Calories 85

Protein 3g

Carbohydrate 11g

Sugars 10g

Fat 3g

Saturates 1g

variation

For a spicier version, add 1 roughly chopped onion with the cucumber in step 1 and add 1–2 deseeded, finely chopped fresh chillies to the garnishes.

cook's tip

This is a perfect soup to have on a summer picnic. Add the ice cubes to the soup before transferring it to a large flask.

1 Put the cucumber, peppers, garlic and basil in a food processor and process for 1½ minutes. Add the passata, olive oil and both kinds of vinegar and process again until smooth.

2 Pour in the vegetable stock and lemon juice and stir. Transfer the mixture to a large bowl. Season to taste with salt and pepper. Cover with clingfilm and leave to chill in the refrigerator for at least 2 hours.

3 To serve, prepare the cucumber, onion and peppers, then place in small serving dishes or arrange decoratively on a plate. Place ice cubes in 4 large soup bowls. Stir the soup and ladle it into the bowls. Garnish with the basil sprigs and serve with the prepared vegetables and chunks of fresh crusty bread.

fragrant chicken soup

This fiery soup is very popular in Thailand, where it is often sold from roadside stalls as a snack. If you prefer a milder flavour, reduce the number of chillies or choose a milder variety.

INGREDIENTS

2 lemon grass stalks

400 ml/14 fl oz coconut milk

3 kaffir lime leaves, torn into small pieces

5-cm/2-inch piece galangal or fresh root ginger, sliced

700 ml/1¼ pints water

500 g/1 lb 2 oz skinless, boneless chicken breasts, trimmed of all visible fat and cut into thin strips

225 g/8 oz shiitake mushrooms, chopped

2 tomatoes, cut into wedges

3 fresh bird's eye chillies, deseeded and thinly sliced

3 tbsp lime juice

2 tbsp Thai fish sauce (nam pla)

fresh coriander leaves, to garnish

NUTRITIONAL INFORMATION

Calories 190

Protein 30g

Carbohydrate 8g

Sugars 7g

Fat 5g

Saturates 2g

variation

You could also make this soup with peeled, raw tiger prawns or, for a vegetarian alternative, use cubes of firm tofu instead of the chicken strips.

cook's tip

Be careful when handling fresh chillies, as they can burn. Wearing rubber gloves is a wise precaution and you should always wash your hands thoroughly afterwards.

1 Prepare the lemon grass. Remove the tough outer leaves and, using a sharp knife, slice diagonally into chunks.

2 Pour the coconut milk into a large, heavy-based saucepan, add the lemon grass, kaffir lime leaves and galangal. Bring to the boil, then reduce the heat and simmer for 2 minutes. Add the water and bring back to the boil. Add the chicken strips, mushrooms and tomatoes and simmer for 5 minutes, or until the chicken strips are tender.

3 Stir in the chillies, lime juice and Thai fish sauce. Using a slotted spoon, remove and discard the lemon grass and galangal. Ladle the soup into 4 large, warmed soup bowls, garnish with a few fresh coriander leaves and serve immediately.

prawn-filled artichokes

serves 4　　　　**prep: 15 mins,** plus 10 mins cooling　　　　**cook: 40–50 mins**

Globe artichokes filled with a delicious stir-fried mix of prawns, garlic, tomatoes and spring onions make an attractive and adventurous starter for a dinner party.

INGREDIENTS

6 tbsp lemon juice

4 globe artichokes

1 tbsp olive or sunflower oil

6 spring onions, finely chopped

1 garlic clove, finely chopped

350 g/12 oz raw prawns, peeled

6 tomatoes, peeled, deseeded and diced

grated rind of 1 lemon

salt and pepper

grated lemon zest, to garnish

NUTRITIONAL INFORMATION

Calories 172

Protein 25g

Carbohydrate 9g

Sugars 7g

Fat 5g

Saturates 1g

variation

If raw prawns are not available, use cooked ones instead. Heat them just long enough to warm them through.

1 Fill a large bowl with cold water and add 2 tablespoons of lemon juice.

2 Working on one artichoke at a time, twist off the stalks, cut the bases flat and pull off any small, tough base leaves. Slice off the tops and trim the tips of the leaves with kitchen scissors. Place in the acidulated water.

3 Bring a large saucepan of water to the boil, add the remaining lemon juice and the artichokes, cover and cook for 30–40 minutes, or until a leaf comes away easily from the bases. Remove from the pan and invert to drain. Set aside to cool.

4 Heat the olive oil in a large frying pan or preheated wok over a medium–high heat. Add the finely chopped spring onions and garlic and stir-fry for 3–4 minutes, then add the prawns and stir-fry for a further 3 minutes, or until they change colour. Stir in the diced tomatoes and lemon rind and season to taste with salt and pepper. Remove the frying pan from the heat.

5 When the artichokes are cool enough to handle, remove and discard the chokes. Spoon the stir-fried prawns into the centre of the artichokes and garnish with grated lemon zest. Serve warm.

antipasto mushrooms

⏲ **cook: 30 mins**   🕐 **prep: 10 mins, plus 30 mins cooling**   **serves 4**

Traditionally, porcini mushrooms, also known as ceps, would be used for this dish, but you can make it with any of your favourite varieties, such as oyster, chanterelles and even button mushrooms.

NUTRITIONAL INFORMATION

Calories	100
Protein	3g
Carbohydrate	2g
Sugars	2g
Fat	9g
Saturates	1g

INGREDIENTS

3 tbsp olive oil

2 garlic cloves, finely chopped

225 g/8 oz tomatoes, peeled, deseeded and finely chopped

1 tbsp finely chopped fresh oregano

salt and pepper

500 g/1 lb 2 oz open-cap and closed cup mushrooms

fresh flat-leaved parsley sprigs, to garnish

crusty bread, to serve

cook's tip

If you want to use dried porcini mushrooms, soak 15 g/ ½ oz mushrooms in boiling water for 20 minutes, or until soft. Drain, then add to the rest of the mushrooms in the frying pan in Step 2.

1 Heat 1 tablespoon of the olive oil in a large, heavy-based saucepan, add the garlic and cook over a low heat, stirring constantly, for 1 minute. Add the tomatoes and oregano and season to taste with salt and pepper. Cook over a low heat, stirring frequently, for 20 minutes, or until the mixture is pulpy and thickened.

2 Using a sharp knife, slice the mushrooms thinly. Heat the remaining olive oil in a large frying pan. Add the mushrooms and cook over a medium heat, stirring frequently, for 5 minutes, or until tender. Stir the mushrooms into the tomato mixture and season with salt. Reduce the heat, cover and simmer for a further 10 minutes.

3 Transfer the mushroom mixture to a bowl and leave to cool. Transfer to a large serving dish, garnish with flat-leaved parsley and serve at room temperature with crusty bread.

mexican vegetable platter

serves 4 **prep: 10 mins,** plus 40 mins chilling **cook: 8 mins**

Known as pico de gallo, *this tempting selection of chilled vegetables and fruit is served with a spicy red pepper and chilli purée. It makes a refreshing starter to a summer supper.*

INGREDIENTS

2 tsp sunflower or corn oil

1 red pepper, deseeded and diced

juice of 1 small orange

juice of 1 lime

1–2 fresh red chillies, deseeded and finely chopped

200 g/7 oz carrots

1 cucumber

½ pineapple

1 mango

½ bunch of fresh mint

NUTRITIONAL INFORMATION

Calories 96

Protein 2g

Carbohydrate 19g

Sugars 18g

Fat 2g

Saturates 0g

---

variation

Other vegetables and fruit can be used. Include slices of avocado, brushed with lime juice to prevent discoloration, and chunks of papaya.

---

cook's tip

Choose firm, slightly underripe mangoes, which slice easily. Using a sharp knife, peel the mango completely, then carefully slice around the stone.

1 First, make the pepper purée. Heat the sunflower oil in a large frying pan and add the pepper. Cook over a medium heat, stirring occasionally for 2 minutes. Add the orange and lime juice and cook for a further 5 minutes. Remove from the heat and leave to cool slightly, then transfer to a blender or food processor and process until a smooth purée forms. Transfer to a small serving bowl and add the chopped chillies. Cover with clingfilm and chill in the refrigerator until ready to serve.

2 Peel the carrots and cut into thin diagonal slices. Peel the cucumber, cut in half and, using a teaspoon, scoop out the seeds, then thinly slice.

3 Cut the plume off the pineapple and discard. Cut the pineapple into quarters, lengthways. Stand the quarters upright and cut away the central core. Slice off the skin with a sharp knife, remove any eyes and cut into cubes. Peel the mango and slice the flesh. Discard the stone. Arrange the fruit and vegetables decoratively on a large serving plate. Cover and leave to chill in the refrigerator for 15 minutes.

4 Slice or tear the mint leaves into thin strips. Spoon the pepper purée over the chilled vegetables, sprinkle with the mint and serve.

crudités with garlic chive & coriander dip

serves 4   **prep: 10 mins** ☾   **cook: 2 mins** ♨

Raw vegetables are the ideal healthy start to a meal, but creamy dips can undo all your good intentions. This is the perfect solution – all the richness and flavour, but none of the fat.

INGREDIENTS

CRUDITÉS

115 g/4 oz baby corn cobs

115 g/4 oz young asparagus spears or sprue, trimmed

1 head of chicory, leaves separated

1 red pepper, deseeded and sliced

1 orange pepper, deseeded and sliced

8 radishes, trimmed

DIP

1 tbsp hot water

1 tsp saffron threads

225 g/8 oz fat-free fromage frais

3 tbsp chopped fresh coriander

1 tbsp snipped fresh garlic chives

salt and pepper

fresh coriander sprigs, to garnish

NUTRITIONAL INFORMATION

Calories 67

Protein 7g

Carbohydrate 9g

Sugars 8g

Fat 1g

Saturates 0g

variation

Try using different selections of vegetables, such as celery sticks, trimmed spring onions, strips of cucumber and carrot batons.

cook's tip

The fat content of fromage frais ranges between 0 and 8 per cent. This is reflected in the consistency. Fat-free fromage frais is great for dips because it is soft and easily mixed with other ingredients.

1 Blanch the corn and asparagus in separate saucepans of boiling water for 2 minutes. Drain, plunge into iced water and drain again. Arrange all the vegetables on a serving platter and cover with a damp tea towel.

2 For the dip, put the water in a small bowl. Lightly crush the saffron threads between your fingers and add to the bowl, then leave to stand for 3–4 minutes, or until the water is a rich golden colour.

3 Put the fromage frais into a separate bowl and beat until smooth, then beat in the infused saffron water. Stir in the chopped coriander and snipped chives and season to taste with salt and pepper. Transfer to a serving bowl and garnish with a few sprigs of fresh coriander. Serve immediately with the prepared vegetables.

chicken & asparagus timbales

serves 4 **prep: 15–20 mins,** ⟲ **plus 1 hr 10 mins chilling** **cook: 30 mins** 🍲

These elegant little moulds would make a wonderful starter for a dinner party. They are packed with flavour, yet light and melt-in-the-mouth, and they look quite stunning. Although they take some time and effort to prepare, the results are worth it.

INGREDIENTS

1 lemon	115 g/4 oz young asparagus spears
2 skinless, boneless chicken	or sprue, trimmed
breasts, about 115 g/4 oz each,	2 tbsp white wine
trimmed of all visible fat	1 sachet powdered gelatine
2 fresh tarragon sprigs	100 g/3½ oz fat-free fromage frais
150 ml/5 fl oz water	1 tsp chopped fresh tarragon
salt and pepper	

NUTRITIONAL INFORMATION

Calories	92
Protein	. . . . .15g
Carbohydrate	. . . . .2g
Sugars	. . . . .2g
Fat	. . . . .2g
Saturates	. . . . .1g

variation

Substitute fresh rosemary or thyme instead of tarragon, but use them sparingly as they have an intense flavour and may overwhelm the dish.

cook's tip

When heating gelatine over a saucepan of simmering water, make sure the gelatine does not boil as it will become stringy and will spoil the finished dish.

1 Cut a strip of rind from the lemon. Squeeze the juice and reserve. Put the lemon rind, chicken, tarragon sprigs and water in a saucepan and season to taste. Cover, bring to the boil, then reduce the heat to low and cook for 20 minutes, or until the meat is tender. Remove the chicken with a slotted spoon and cool. Sieve and reserve the cooking

liquid. Blanch the asparagus for 5 minutes. Drain, then cut off and reserve 4 cm/1½ inches of the tips. Chop the stalks.

2 Put the reserved cooking liquid in a measuring jug. Make up to 150 ml/5 fl oz with water, if necessary. Stir in the wine. Put 4 tablespoons of the mixture in a heatproof bowl, sprinkle

½ teaspoon of gelatine on top, leave for 2 minutes, then set over a saucepan of simmering water. Stir for 2–3 minutes. Divide between 4 ramekins and chill for 5 minutes. Arrange 2 asparagus tips, facing in opposite directions, in each ramekin and chill until set. Dissolve the remaining gelatine in the remaining stock and wine, as before.

3 Chop the chicken, then process in a food processor until smooth. Add the lemon juice, fromage frais and gelatine mixture and mix briefly. Transfer to a bowl, stir in the asparagus stalks and tarragon and season. Divide between the ramekins and chill for 1 hour, or until set. Dip the base of the ramekins in hot water and invert onto 4 plates.

chinese pot stickers

serves 6　　　　　**prep: 30 mins**　　　　　**cook: 50-60 mins**

These tasty chicken- and vegetable-filled dumplings are equally suitable for serving as part of a Chinese meal or as a starter before a Western main course. You can also serve them with plain dark soy sauce or chilli sauce for dipping, if you like.

INGREDIENTS

175 g/6 oz Chinese leaves, shredded

1 litre/1¾ pints boiling water

115 g/4 oz lean chicken mince

5 canned water chestnuts, drained, rinsed and chopped

1 spring onion, finely chopped

1 tablespoon Chinese rice wine

1 teaspoon light soy sauce

1 tsp cornflour

pepper

24 wonton wrappers, thawed if frozen

groundnut or sunflower oil, for brushing

DIPPING SAUCE

125 ml/4 fl oz Vegetable Stock (see page 11)

1 tbsp caster sugar

3 tbsp dark soy sauce

NUTRITIONAL INFORMATION

Calories 109

Protein 7g

Carbohydrate 19g

Sugars 4g

Fat 1g

Saturates 0g

variation

You can substitute the same quantity of lean minced steak or chopped peeled raw prawns for the chicken, if you like.

  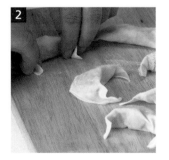

cook's tip

Cook the pot stickers in batches, as they should not touch each other during the process. When steaming, add enough water to come about halfway up the sides of the pot stickers.

1 First make the dipping sauce by mixing all the ingredients in a small bowl, stirring until the sugar has dissolved, and set aside.

2 Put the Chinese leaves in a colander and pour over the boiling water. Drain well, pressing the leaves with the back of a spoon. Transfer the Chinese leaves to a large bowl with the chicken, water chestnuts, spring onion, Chinese rice wine, soy sauce and cornflour. Season to taste with pepper and mix well. Spread out 1 wonton wrapper and place a teaspoon of the filling in the centre. Brush the edge with water and fold to make a half moon. Press the edges together to seal and crimp the rim slightly. Gently curve the dumpling by pinching the ends of the rim between your forefingers and thumbs. Make the remaining dumplings in the same way.

3 Brush the base of a non-stick wok or frying pan with groundnut oil and set over a medium heat. Add 5–6 dumplings in a single layer, smooth sides downwards. Cook for 2–3 minutes, or until golden brown underneath. Add 3–4 tablespoons water, partially cover and steam for 10 minutes, or until cooked through and most of the water has evaporated. Transfer to a serving plate and keep warm. Cook the remaining dumplings, in batches, in the same way. Serve with the dipping sauce.

asparagus with orange dressing

serves 4   **prep: 10 mins,**   **cook: 10 mins**
plus 15 mins standing

Asparagus is in season for only a short time and is a special treat in late spring and early summer. Imported asparagus is available all year round, but it may be very expensive.

INGREDIENTS

2 oranges

350 g/12 oz asparagus, trimmed

1 tablespoon lemon juice

1 spring onion, finely chopped

1 garlic clove, finely chopped

2 tbsp extra virgin olive oil

1 tbsp white wine vinegar

NUTRITIONAL INFORMATION

Calories 88

Protein 3g

Carbohydrate 6g

Sugars 6g

Fat 6g

Saturates 1g

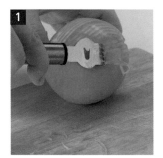

cook's tip

A special asparagus kettle is designed so that the stems cook in the water while the tips are steamed. If you don't have one, use a deep saucepan, tie the asparagus loosely and wedge upright.

1 Bring a small saucepan of water to the boil over a medium heat. Using a zester, cut the rind of both oranges into very thin strips. Reserve the oranges. Add the rind to the saucepan, return the mixture to the boil and simmer for 1 minute. Drain the rind, refresh under cold running water and drain again, then set aside.

2 Bring a large saucepan of water to the boil over a medium heat. Add the asparagus and cook for 5 minutes, or until just tender. Drain the asparagus, refresh under cold running water and drain again. Pat dry with kitchen paper. Arrange the asparagus on a serving dish, cover and chill in the refrigerator until required.

3 To make the orange dressing, squeeze the reserved oranges to make 5 tablespoons of orange juice. Mix the orange juice, lemon juice, spring onion, garlic and orange rind together in a small bowl, then leave to stand at room temperature for 15 minutes to allow the flavours to mingle. Using a balloon whisk, whisk in the olive oil and vinegar. Pour the dressing over the asparagus and serve immediately.

parma ham with figs

⏲ **cook: 0 mins**

◔ **prep: 10 mins, plus 20 mins chilling**

serves 4

This classic Italian starter couldn't be easier or more delicious. Parma ham has a uniquely aromatic flavour and is served in paper-thin slices. Succulent fresh figs make a natural partnership.

NUTRITIONAL INFORMATION

Calories	124
Protein	. . . . .13g
Carbohydrate	. . . . .6g
Sugars	. . . . .5g
Fat	. . . . .6g
Saturates	. . . . .2g

INGREDIENTS

175 g/6 oz Parma ham, thinly sliced

pepper

4 fresh figs

1 lime

2 fresh basil sprigs

variation

This dish is also delicious made with 4 slices of charentais melon or 12–16 cooked and cooled asparagus spears, instead of the figs.

 1 Using a sharp knife, trim the visible fat from the slices of ham and discard. Arrange the ham on 4 large serving plates, loosely folding it so that it falls into decorative shapes. Season to taste with pepper.

2 Using a sharp knife, cut each fig lengthways into 4 wedges. Arrange a fig on each serving plate. Cut the lime into 6 wedges, place a wedge on each plate and reserve the others. Remove the leaves from the basil sprigs and divide between the plates. Cover with clingfilm and leave in the refrigerator to chill until ready to serve.

3 Just before serving, remove the plates from the refrigerator and squeeze the juice from the remaining lime wedges over the ham.

crab cakes with salsa verde

serves 4　　　　**prep: 15 mins,**　　　**cook: 15 mins**
plus 30–60 mins chilling

These spicy fish cakes are popular throughout Thailand, where they are eaten as between-meal snacks. Mixing crabmeat with white fish makes the cakes easier to handle and the dish more economical.

INGREDIENTS

250 g/9 oz crabmeat, thawed if frozen

250 g/9 oz white fish fillet, such as cod, skinned and roughly chopped

1 fresh red chilli, deseeded and roughly chopped

1 garlic clove, roughly chopped

2.5-cm/1-inch piece of fresh root ginger, roughly chopped

1 lemon grass stalk, roughly chopped

3 tbsp chopped fresh coriander

1 egg white

groundnut or sunflower oil, for frying

SALSA VERDE

2 fresh green chillies, deseeded and roughly chopped

8 spring onions, roughly chopped

2 garlic cloves, roughly chopped

1 bunch of fresh parsley

grated rind and juice of 1 lime

juice of 1 lemon

4 tbsp olive oil

1 tbsp green Tabasco sauce

salt and pepper

NUTRITIONAL INFORMATION

Calories 318

Protein 26g

Carbohydrate 2g

Sugars 1g

Fat 23g

Saturates 3g

variation

For an elegant presentation, garnish the crab cakes with fresh Chinese chives. If these are unavailable, use ordinary fresh chives instead.

cook's tip

Much of the fat in this recipe is contained in the salsa verde dip, so if you would prefer a lower-fat dish, serve only small helpings of the salsa verde. The remainder can be stored in the refrigerator.

1 Place the crabmeat, fish, red chilli, garlic, ginger, lemon grass, coriander and egg white in a food processor and process until thoroughly blended, then transfer to a bowl, cover with clingfilm and chill in the refrigerator for 30–60 minutes.

2 Meanwhile, make the salsa verde. Put the green chillies, spring onions, garlic and parsely in a food processor and process until finely chopped. Transfer to a small bowl and stir in the lime rind, lime and lemon juice, olive oil and green Tabasco sauce. Season to taste with salt and pepper, cover with clingfilm and leave to chill in the refrigerator until ready to serve.

3 Heat 2 tablespoons of the groundnut oil in a non-stick frying pan. Add spoonfuls of the crab mixture, flattening them gently with a spatula and keeping them spaced well apart. Cook for 4 minutes, then turn with a spatula and cook the other side for 3 minutes, or until golden brown. Remove from the frying pan and keep warm while you cook the remaining batches, adding more oil if necessary. Transfer the crab cakes to a large serving plate, garnish and serve with the salsa verde.

trout mousse

serves 6 **prep: 15 mins,** plus **3 hrs 20 mins chilling** **cook: 15 mins**

This delicate pink mousse makes a superb starter for a dinner party or buffet table. Trout is an oily fish, but contains the 'good' omega-3 essential fatty acids that are vital for wellbeing and protect against heart disease and circulatory problems.

INGREDIENTS

150 ml/5 fl oz Fish Stock (see page 11)
1 tbsp French vermouth
1 tbsp lime juice
1 small onion, finely chopped
250 g/9 oz trout fillets
1 tsp tomato purée
2 tbsp Greek-style yogurt

salt and white pepper
1½ tsp water
½ sachet (1½ tsp) powdered gelatine
1 large egg white
fresh dill sprigs, to garnish
Melba toast (see Cook's Tip) or toasted wholemeal bread, to serve

NUTRITIONAL INFORMATION

Calories 79

Protein 10g

Carbohydrate 1g

Sugars 1g

Fat 4g

Saturates 1g

variation

This mousse can also be made with sea trout fillets, which also have pink flesh and a delicate flavour.

cook's tip

To make Melba toast, remove the crusts from slices of bread and grill on both sides. Slice through horizontally to give 2 very thin slices. Cut in half diagonally and grill until golden.

1 Pour the fish stock into a wide, shallow pan and add the vermouth, lime juice and onion. Bring to the boil, then reduce the heat to low and simmer for 3 minutes. Add the fish fillets, skin-side down, cover and poach for 3 minutes. Remove from the heat and leave, still covered, until cool. Lift out the fish, reserving the stock, then remove and discard the skin and flake the flesh. Sieve the stock into a food processor, add the fish and process until a smooth paste forms. Transfer to a bowl and beat in the tomato purée and yogurt. Season to taste.

2 Pour the water into a small, heatproof bowl and sprinkle the gelatine on

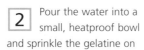

the surface. Leave to stand for 2 minutes to soften, then set the bowl over a saucepan of simmering water and stir for 2–3 minutes, or until the gelatine has dissolved. Pour the gelatine mixture into the fish mixture in a steady stream, beating constantly. Chill in the refrigerator for 15–20 minutes, or until just beginning to set.

3 Whisk the egg white until stiff, but not dry. Gently stir one-quarter of the egg white into the fish mixture, then fold in the remainder. Rinse 6 ramekin dishes or bowls with water and spoon in the fish mixture. Smooth the tops, cover and chill in the refrigerator for 2–3 hours, or until set. Garnish with dill sprigs and serve with toast.

artichoke hearts with a warm dressing

serves 4   **prep: 15 mins** ⏱   **cook: 45 mins** ⏱

Artichoke hearts are truly a luxury and taste superb with this warm, nutty dressing. For less fat content, omit the walnut garnish.

INGREDIENTS

250 g/9 oz mixed salad leaves, such as

lollo rosso, escarole and lamb's lettuce

6 tbsp lemon juice

4 globe artichokes

5 tbsp Calvados

1 shallot, very finely chopped

pinch of salt

1 tbsp red wine vinegar

3 tbsp walnut oil

TO GARNISH

55 g/2 oz shelled walnuts, chopped

1 tbsp finely chopped fresh parsley

NUTRITIONAL INFORMATION

Calories 287

Protein 7g

Carbohydrate 14g

Sugars 2g

Fat 18g

Saturates 2g

variation

This recipe also works well with good quality canned or bottled artichoke hearts. Drain and rinse well before using.

1 Place the salad leaves in a bowl and set aside. Fill a bowl with cold water and add 2 tablespoons of the lemon juice. Working on one artichoke at a time, twist off the stalks, cut the bases flat and pull off all the dark outer leaves. Slice the artichokes in half horizontally and discard the top parts. Trim around the bases to remove the outer dark green layer and place in the acidulated water. Bring a saucepan of water to the boil, add the remaining lemon juice and the artichokes, cover and cook for 30–40 minutes, or until tender. Drain, refresh under cold running water and drain again. Pull off and discard the remaining leaves, slice off and discard the chokes and set the hearts aside.

2 Pour the Calvados into a small saucepan, add the shallot and salt and bring to just below boiling point. Reduce the heat, carefully ignite the Calvados and continue to cook until the flames have died down. Stir in the vinegar and walnut oil and cook, stirring constantly, for 1 minute. Remove the saucepan from the heat.

3 Spoon half the dressing over the salad leaves and toss well to coat. Transfer the salad leaves to a large serving plate and top with the artichoke hearts. Spoon the remaining dressing over the artichoke hearts, garnish with the walnuts and parsley and serve immediately.

oysters rockefeller

⏲ **cook: 9 mins**   ⏱ **prep: 30 mins**   **serves 6**

This is a variation of the famous New Orleans dish, which is cooked and served on a bed of rock salt. Although an extravagant indulgence, it makes a spectacular starter for a special occasion.

NUTRITIONAL INFORMATION	
Calories	.97
Protein	13g
Carbohydrate	6g
Sugars	3g
Fat	2g
Saturates	0g

INGREDIENTS

450 g/1 lb fresh spinach leaves

rock salt

36 fresh oysters in their shells

4 spring onions, chopped

2 celery sticks, chopped

3 fresh parsley sprigs

1–2 tbsp low-fat natural yogurt

pinch of cayenne pepper

1 tbsp pastis (see Cook's Tip)

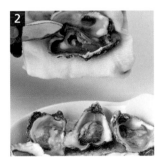

cook's tip

Pastis is an alcoholic drink which is flavoured with star anise. It is very popular in the south of France. The best-known brand is Pernod.

1 Preheat the oven to 230°C/450°F/Gas Mark 8. Trim the stalks from the spinach leaves and rinse the leaves under cold running water. Put the wet leaves into a large saucepan, then cover and cook over a medium heat for 3 minutes. Turn the spinach over, cover and cook for a further 2 minutes. Drain well, squeezing out as much liquid as possible, then set aside. Cover the bases of 2 ovenproof dishes with a 1-cm/½-inch layer of rock salt.

2 Wrap a tea towel around one hand and grasp an oyster, flat shell uppermost. Insert a strong knife into the hinge between the shells and twist to prise them open. Run the blade along the inside of the top shell to sever the upper muscle, then along the inside of the lower shell to cut the lower muscle. Discard the top shells. Shuck the remaining oysters in the same way. Set the shells on the salt layers.

3 Place the spinach, spring onions, celery, parsley, yogurt and cayenne pepper in a food processor and pulse until a smooth purée forms. Transfer to a bowl and stir in the pastis. Cover each oyster with a spoonful of the spinach purée, then bake in the preheated oven for 4 minutes. Serve immediately.

snacks & light meals

There are many occasions when we feel it is time for a 'little something',

but don't want a complete meal. Many popular snacks and easy 'instant' meals – from crisps

and biscuits to pizzas and sausages – are extremely high in fat (as well as salt and sugar),

and it is all too easy to wreck your healthy eating plan. So turn to this chapter, packed with

delicious low-fat snacks and light meals, to solve the problem. There is something for everyone.

Need a quick snack to keep you going in the middle of the day? Try one of the

luscious Scrumptious Sandwiches (see page 48). If the kids come home from school starving and

it's a long way until supper time, make a batch of Falafel (see page 66). Want a light lunch

for guests? How about Cantaloupe & Crab Salad (see page 72)? Need to fuel the family

for an action-packed weekend? Try Mexican Eggs (see page 58). Many of these dishes are also

perfect for school lunch boxes and picnics. Whether you want a hot dish to fill the gap on

a wintery day or to ring the changes with some unusual summer salads,

you are sure to find the perfect healthy choice.

pasta with low-fat pesto

serves 4   **prep: 5 mins**   **cook: 8–10 mins**

Pesto is a wonderfully useful sauce that can be served with all kinds of foods, from pasta to baked potatoes, but its great disadvantage is that it contains over 50 g/1¾ oz fat per serving. You can make this sauce without the addition of lots of olive oil, thus reducing its fat content to one-quarter of that of traditional pesto.

INGREDIENTS

225 g/8 oz dried spaghetti or linguine

fresh basil sprigs, to garnish

LOW-FAT PESTO

55 g/2 oz fresh basil leaves

25 g/1 oz fresh flat-leaved
parsley sprigs

1 garlic clove, roughly chopped

25 g/1 oz pine kernels

115 g/4 oz low-fat curd cheese

20 g/¾ oz Parmesan cheese

salt and pepper

NUTRITIONAL INFORMATION

Calories 288

Protein 15g

Carbohydrate 44g

Sugars 3g

Fat 7g

Saturates 1g

variation

You could substitute pecorino – Italian ewe's milk cheese – for the Parmesan cheese, if you like.

cook's tip

If the pesto is too thick, you can dilute it with a little of the pasta cooking water, but remember to reserve the water when you drain the pasta.

1 Bring a large saucepan of lightly salted water to the boil over a medium heat. Add the pasta, return to the boil and cook for 8–10 minutes, or until tender but still firm to the bite.

2 Meanwhile, make the pesto. Put half the basil, half the parsley, the garlic, pine kernels and curd cheese into a food processor and process until smooth. Add the remaining basil and parsley, then grate and add the Parmesan cheese. Season to taste with salt and pepper. Process again briefly.

3 Drain the cooked pasta and return to the saucepan. Add the pesto to the pasta and toss thoroughly with 2 forks. Transfer to 4 large, warmed serving plates, garnish with a few sprigs of fresh basil and serve.

fettuccine with smoked salmon

serves 4   **prep: 5 mins**   **cook: 10 mins**

This simple dish takes just moments to make, looks lovely, tastes fabulous and contains absolutely no saturated fat – what more could you possibly want?

INGREDIENTS

salt and pepper

225 g/8 oz dried fettuccine

1 tsp olive oil

1 garlic clove, finely chopped

55 g/2 oz smoked salmon, cut into thin strips

55 g/2 oz watercress leaves, plus extra to garnish

NUTRITIONAL INFORMATION

Calories 222

Protein 11g

Carbohydrate 42g

Sugars 2g

Fat 3g

Saturates 0g

variation

Substitute the same amount of rocket for the watercress, if you like, and garnish with a few sprigs of fresh flat-leaved parsley.

cook's tip

You can often buy misshapen offcuts of smoked salmon for a fraction of the price of neat smoked salmon slices in some large supermarkets.

1 Bring a large saucepan of lightly salted water to the boil over a medium heat. Add the pasta, return to the boil and cook for 8–10 minutes, or until tender but still firm to the bite.

2 Meanwhile, heat the olive oil in a large non-stick frying pan. Add the garlic and cook over a low heat, stirring constantly, for 30 seconds. Add the salmon and watercress, season to taste with pepper and cook for a further 30 seconds, or until the watercress has wilted.

3 Drain the cooked pasta and return to the saucepan. Mix the salmon and watercress with the pasta. Toss the mixture thoroughly using 2 large forks. Divide between 4 large serving plates and garnish with extra watercress leaves. Serve immediately.

scrumptious sandwiches

Use your favourite type of bread or rolls, such as Granary, sourdough or rye, for these delicious sandwich fillings.

INGREDIENTS

2 slices bread or 1 roll

TUNA AND WATERCRESS FILLING

2 tbsp canned tuna in brine, drained

2 tbsp finely chopped watercress

1 tbsp canned sweetcorn, drained

2 tbsp Mayonnaise (see page 12)

½ tsp Dijon mustard

dash of lemon juice

salt and pepper

PRAWN AND COTTAGE CHEESE FILLING

2 tbsp low-fat cottage cheese

¼ tsp tomato purée

pepper

6 cooked, peeled prawns

1 button mushroom, thinly sliced

2–3 slices red pepper

1 fresh chive, snipped

CHICKEN FILLING

1 tbsp fat-free fromage frais

1–2 Webbs lettuce leaves, shredded

25 g/1 oz cooked chicken, skinned and cut into thin strips

¼ tsp Dijon mustard

½ celery stick, sliced

3 shelled pistachio nuts, sliced

salt and pepper

NUTRITIONAL INFORMATION

Calories 296/250/260

Protein 22/22/19g

Carbohydrate 42/35/36g

Sugars 6/5/6g

Fat 6/3/5g

Saturates 2/1/1g

---

variation

Following the tuna recipe, replace the fish with crab meat, the watercress with lettuce and the mustard with 1 teaspoon snipped chilli.

cook's tip

If you are not going to eat the sandwich immediately, wrap it loosely in clingfilm or greaseproof paper and store in the refrigerator.

1 To make the tuna and watercress filling, put all the ingredients in a large mixing bowl and, using a metal spoon, stir until thoroughly combined. Spread the tuna mixture evenly over 1 slice of bread or half a roll, then season to taste with salt and pepper and top with the remaining slice or half roll. Serve immediately.

2 To make the prawn and cottage cheese filling, place the cottage cheese in a small bowl, stir in the tomato purée and season to taste with pepper. Spread the cheese mixture over 1 slice of bread or half a roll and top with the cooked prawns and slices of mushroom and pepper. Sprinkle with the snipped chive and top with the remaining slice of bread or half roll. Serve immediately.

3 To make the chicken filling, spread the fromage frais over 1 slice of bread or half a roll and place the lettuce on top. Toss the chicken with the mustard in a small bowl and arrange over the lettuce, then top with the celery and nuts and season to taste with salt and pepper. Top with the remaining slice of bread or half roll.

spicy chicken with naan

serves 4　　　　**prep: 10 mins,** ⏲ **plus 1–2 hrs marinating**　　　　**cook: 20 mins** ⏲

This easy Indian-style dish makes a delicious lunch or supper and can be served with additional salad, if you like. It is also excellent served cold. Make mini chicken naan for children's lunch boxes.

INGREDIENTS

450 g/1 lb skinless, boneless chicken, trimmed of all visible fat and cut into 2.5-cm/½-inch cubes

4 naan breads

½ onion, sliced into rings

2 tomatoes, thinly sliced

¼ iceberg lettuce, shredded

MARINADE

3 tbsp low-fat natural yogurt

1 tsp garam masala

1 tsp chilli powder

2 tbsp lime juice

2 tbsp chopped fresh coriander

1 fresh red chilli, deseeded and finely chopped

salt and pepper

NUTRITIONAL INFORMATION

Calories 503

Protein 42g

Carbohydrate 72g

Sugars 6g

Fat 15g

Saturates 3g

variation

You could serve the chicken and salad in pitta pockets, if you like. Toast the pitta breads lightly first, then cut a slit with a sharp knife to make a pocket.

cook's tip

To make the chicken less spicy, use just ¼ teaspoon of garam masala and ¼ teaspoon of chilli powder and omit the fresh chilli in the marinade.

1 Place the chicken cubes in a shallow, non-metallic dish. Put all the marinade ingredients in a jug and stir until well blended, seasoning to taste with the salt and pepper. Pour the marinade over the chicken, tossing to coat thoroughly. Cover with clingfilm and leave to marinate in the refrigerator for 1–2 hours.

2 Using a slotted spoon, transfer the chicken to a flameproof dish. Cook under a preheated hot grill, stirring and turning occasionally, for 20 minutes, or until tender and cooked through.

3 Meanwhile, cut a slit in the naan breads to make a pocket. Fill the naan pockets with the cooked chicken, onion rings, tomato slices and shredded lettuce and serve immediately.

turkey patties

serves 4　　　　**prep: 15 mins,**　　　　**cook: 20–25 mins**
plus 30 mins chilling

These savoury patties are served with a colourful beetroot and apple sauce that gives a fabulous boost to the sometimes bland flavour of turkey. The sauce would taste just as good with plain grilled or griddled turkey breasts.

INGREDIENTS

1½ tsp sunflower or corn oil	2 tbsp chopped fresh basil
55 g/2 oz spinach, shredded	40 g/1½ oz dried breadcrumbs
2 garlic cloves, finely chopped	salt and pepper
225 g/8 oz skinless, boneless turkey	fresh dill sprigs, to garnish
breast, trimmed of all visible fat and	
finely chopped	**SAUCE**
6 tbsp cold mashed potato	1 peeled, cooked beetroot, finely diced
175 g/6 oz low-fat cottage	300 ml/10 fl oz apple purée or
cheese, strained	unsweetened apple sauce
3 spring onions, chopped	1 tsp Dijon mustard
1 tsp wholegrain mustard	1 tsp snipped fresh dill

variation

If you are planning to cook the beetroot for the sauce yourself, you could use the green tops as a substitute for the spinach.

cook's tip

Dampen your hands slightly before forming the mixture into patties to prevent it from sticking to your fingers. To make it easier for coating, put the breadcrumbs on a plate and roll the patties in them.

1 Preheat the oven to 190°C/375°F/Gas Mark 5. To make the sauce, mix all the ingredients together in a bowl, cover with clingfilm and leave to chill in the refrigerator until required. Alternatively, put all the ingredients in a food processor and process until smooth, then transfer to a small bowl, cover and chill in the refrigerator until required.

2 To make the patties, heat the oil in a non-stick frying pan. Add the spinach and garlic, then cover and cook over a low heat for 2 minutes, or until the spinach has wilted. Remove from the heat and leave to cool. When cool, place in a bowl and mix with the turkey, potato, cottage cheese, spring onions, mustard, basil and half the

breadcrumbs. Season to taste with salt and pepper. Form the mixture into 8 patties, about 1-cm/½-inch thick. Coat with the remaining breadcrumbs.

3 Place the patties on a baking tray and bake in the preheated oven for 15–20 minutes, or until golden brown. Transfer to 4 warmed serving plates, add

a spoonful of sauce to each plate and top with a fresh dill sprig. Serve immediately.

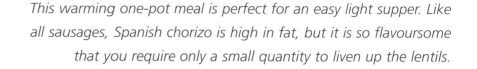

sausage & lentil stew

serves 4　　　　　　**prep: 5 mins**　　　　　　**cook: 1 hr**

This warming one-pot meal is perfect for an easy light supper. Like all sausages, Spanish chorizo is high in fat, but it is so flavoursome that you require only a small quantity to liven up the lentils.

INGREDIENTS

55 g/2 oz chorizo sausage,
very thinly sliced

1 onion, finely chopped

225 g/8 oz Puy lentils

600 ml/1 pint Chicken Stock
(see page 11)

400 ml/14 fl oz water

1 carrot, thinly sliced

1 celery stick, thinly sliced

2 tsp chopped fresh parsley

salt and pepper

NUTRITIONAL INFORMATION

Calories	.217
Protein	.17g
Carbohydrate	.30g
Sugars	.3g
Fat	.4g
Saturates	.1g

cook's tip

Puy lentils are best for this stew, as they have a fine flavour and hold their shape well when cooked. You could use brown lentils instead, but red split ones would become too mushy.

1 Reserve a few slices of chorizo for the garnish and cut the remaining slices into thin strips. Dry-fry the slices and strips in a frying pan over a low heat, stirring frequently, for 2–3 minutes. Remove the chorizo slices and set aside. Add the onion to the frying pan and cook, stirring occasionally, for a further 5 minutes, or until softened.

2 Transfer the onion to a heavy-based saucepan. Add the lentils, chicken stock and water and bring to the boil over a medium heat. Cover and simmer for 30–40 minutes, or until the lentils are tender.

3 Add the carrot, celery and parsley and season to taste with salt and pepper.

Cover and simmer for a further 8–10 minutes, or until the carrot is tender. Serve immediately, garnished with the reserved chorizo slices.

baked potatoes with pesto chicken

⏲ **cook: 1–1 hr 15 mins**   ⏲ **prep: 5 mins**   **serves 4**

*Filled baked potatoes make wonderful comfort food on a cold day,
but resist the urge to add butter, soured cream or grated cheese.
This potato needs only a green salad to make a delicious light meal.*

NUTRITIONAL INFORMATION

Calories	.250
Protein	.20g
Carbohydrate	.31g
Sugars	.6g
Fat	.6g
Saturates	.1g

INGREDIENTS

4 large potatoes

sunflower or corn oil, for brushing

2 skinless, boneless chicken breasts,
about 115 g/4 oz each, trimmed of
all visible fat

250 ml/9 fl oz low-fat natural yogurt

1 tbsp Low-fat Pesto (see page 44)

green salad, to serve

cook's tip

If you do not have a griddle
pan, cook the chicken under a
preheated hot grill instead,
but leave the skin on to
prevent the flesh from drying
out. Remove the skin before
slicing the chicken.

1 Preheat the oven
to 200°C/400°F/Gas
Mark 6. Prick the potatoes
all over with a fork and bake
in the preheated oven for
1–1¼ hours, or until soft and
cooked through.

2 About 15 minutes
before the potatoes are
ready, heat a griddle pan and
brush with a little sunflower
oil. Add the chicken and cook
over a medium–high heat for
5 minutes on each side, or
until cooked through and
tender. Meanwhile, put the
yogurt and pesto in a bowl
and mix until blended.

3 Slice the potatoes down
the centre, almost right
through, and open out. Cut
the cooked chicken into slices.

Divide the slices between the
potatoes and top with the
yogurt. Transfer to 4 warmed
serving plates and serve with a
green salad.

roast summer vegetables

serves 4   **prep: 10 mins**   **cook: 20–25 mins**

This appetising and colourful mixture of Mediterranean vegetables makes a sensational summer lunch for vegetarians and meat-eaters alike. Roasting brings out the full flavour and sweetness of the peppers, aubergines, courgettes and onions.

INGREDIENTS

2 tbsp olive oil	1 orange pepper
1 fennel bulb	4 garlic cloves
2 red onions	4 fresh rosemary sprigs
2 beef tomatoes	pepper
1 aubergine	crusty bread, to serve (optional)
2 courgettes	
1 yellow pepper	
1 red pepper	

NUTRITIONAL INFORMATION

Calories 142

Protein 4g

Carbohydrate 18g

Sugars 13g

Fat 7g

Saturates 1g

variation

Substitute a herb-flavoured oil, such as tarragon or garlic and rosemary, for the plain olive oil, if you like.

cook's tip

You can also serve this dish as an accompaniment to grilled or barbecued chicken or monkfish. This quantity will serve 8 people.

1 Preheat the oven to 200°C/400°F/Gas Mark 6. Brush a large ovenproof dish with a little of the olive oil. Prepare the vegetables. Cut the fennel, red onions and tomatoes into wedges. Slice the aubergine and courgettes thickly, then deseed all the peppers and cut into chunks. Arrange the vegetables in the dish and tuck the garlic cloves and rosemary sprigs among them. Drizzle with the remaining olive oil and season to taste with pepper.

2 Roast in the preheated oven for 10 minutes. Remove the dish from the oven and turn the vegetables over with a slotted spoon. Return to the oven and roast for a further 10–15 minutes, or until tender and beginning to turn golden brown.

3 Serve the vegetables straight from the dish, or transfer to a warmed serving plate. Serve with crusty bread, if you like.

mexican eggs

serves 4   **prep: 10 mins**   **cook: 50 mins**

This dish is simple to prepare and makes the perfect lunch or light supper. Serve straight from the frying pan with plenty of crisp salad or a selection of freshly steamed vegetables, if you like.

INGREDIENTS

1 tbsp sunflower or corn oil	1 tsp ground cumin
1 red pepper, deseeded and	125 ml/4 fl oz red wine
cut into batons	800 g/1 lb 12 oz canned
1 yellow pepper, deseeded and	chopped tomatoes
cut into batons	1 tsp muscovado sugar
1 garlic clove, finely chopped	salt and pepper
2 fresh red chillies, deseeded and	4 eggs
finely chopped	2 tbsp chopped fresh coriander,
1 tsp ground coriander	to garnish

NUTRITIONAL INFORMATION

Calories 156

Protein 8g

Carbohydrate 7g

Sugars 7g

Fat 8g

Saturates 2g

variation

If you like, omit the chillies and add 115 g/4 oz thinly sliced mushrooms and 225 g/8 oz canned sweetcorn with the tomatoes in Step 2.

cook's tip

Capsaicin – the substance that makes chillies hot – is not found in the seeds, but is concentrated in the flesh surrounding them. Removing the seeds will reduce the heat.

1 Heat the sunflower oil in a large frying pan. Add the peppers and garlic and cook over a medium heat, stirring occasionally, for 2 minutes, or until softened. Stir in the chillies, ground coriander and cumin and cook, stirring, for 1 minute. Pour in the red wine, bring to the boil, reduce the heat to medium and simmer for 3 minutes.

2 Stir in the tomatoes with their juice and the sugar, reduce the heat to low and simmer gently for 20–25 minutes, or until thickened. Season to taste with salt and pepper.

3 Using a large spoon, make 4 hollows in the tomato mixture. Break an egg into each hollow, cover the frying pan and cook for 10–15 minutes, or until set. Sprinkle with chopped fresh coriander and serve.

serves 4 **prep: 10 mins,** ⏱ **cook: 30 mins** 🍲
plus 30 mins soaking

To achieve the authentic creamy texture of risotto, use arborio or carnaroli rice. These shorter-grain varieties can absorb more liquid than long-grain rice, but still retain their 'bite'. They are widely available from supermarkets and may be labelled 'risotto rice'. Avoid easy-cook risotto rice, which will not have the same texture.

NUTRITIONAL INFORMATION

Calories 384

Protein 10g

Carbohydrate 71g

Sugars 2g

Fat 7g

Saturates 2g

INGREDIENTS

15 g/½ oz dried porcini mushrooms

300 ml/10 fl oz boiling water

1 tbsp olive oil

1 onion, finely chopped

1 garlic clove, finely chopped

1 fresh sage sprig, finely chopped

300 g/10½ oz risotto rice

125 ml/4 fl oz white wine

225 g/8 oz chestnut mushrooms, sliced

700 ml/1¼ pints hot Vegetable Stock (see page 11)

4 tbsp freshly grated Parmesan cheese

salt and pepper

shavings of fresh Parmesan cheese, to garnish

variation

Instead of chestnut mushrooms, use field mushrooms. Substitute Chicken Stock (see page 11) for Vegetable Stock, if you like.

cook's tip

Place the stock in a separate saucepan before you start cooking the risotto. Bring to the boil, then reduce the heat and simmer to keep the stock at the right temperature while you add it to the rice.

1 Put the dried porcini mushrooms in a small bowl and pour in the boiling water to cover. Leave to soak for 30 minutes, or until the mushrooms are soft. Drain, reserving the soaking liquid. Using a sharp knife, chop the mushrooms and sieve the soaking liquid through a coffee filter paper or muslin-lined sieve.

2 Heat the olive oil in a large, heavy-based saucepan. Add the onion, garlic and sage and cook, stirring frequently, for 5 minutes. Add the rice and cook over a low heat, stirring constantly to coat the grains with the oil, for 3 minutes. Add the wine and cook, stirring constantly, until it has evaporated. Stir in the porcini and chestnut mushrooms, the mushroom soaking liquid and a large ladleful of the hot vegetable stock. Simmer, stirring constantly, until all the stock has been absorbed. Continue adding stock and stirring in this way for 20 minutes, or until all the stock has been absorbed and the rice is tender but still firm to the bite.

3 Remove the saucepan from the heat, stir in the Parmesan cheese and season to taste with salt and pepper. Divide the risotto between 4 warmed serving plates, garnish with shavings of Parmesan cheese and serve.

vegetable samosas

serves 4 **prep: 30 mins** **cook: 35–40 mins**

Everyone will love these hot and spicy vegetable samosas as they are oven-baked rather than deep-fried. Serve either hot or cold with mango chutney as an appetizer or as part of a light lunch. They are also perfect as a snack at any time of the day.

INGREDIENTS

1 small potato, peeled and quartered

1 small carrot, halved

4 cauliflower florets

1 tsp sunflower or corn oil, plus extra for brushing

2 tsp lime juice

1 tbsp water

1 shallot, finely chopped

3 tbsp frozen peas

1 fresh green chilli, deseeded and finely chopped

½ tsp cumin seeds

½ tsp black cumin seeds

½ tsp ground turmeric

½ tsp ground coriander

beaten egg, to glaze

mango chutney, to serve

PASTRY

40 g/1½ oz malted flour

125 g/4½ oz plain flour, plus extra for dusting

40 g/1½ oz sunflower margarine

50–75 ml/2–2½ fl oz skimmed milk

NUTRITIONAL INFORMATION

Calories	.139
Protein	.4g
Carbohydrate	.19g
Sugars	.2g
Fat	.6g
Saturates	.2g

variation

If you would like these samosas to taste a little spicier, use 2 fresh green chillies, deseeded and finely chopped, instead of just one.

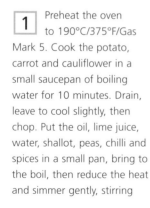

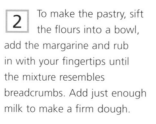

cook's tip

If you have time, wrap the dough in foil and leave to chill in the refrigerator for 15–30 minutes before you roll it out.

1 Preheat the oven to 190°C/375°F/Gas Mark 5. Cook the potato, carrot and cauliflower in a small saucepan of boiling water for 10 minutes. Drain, leave to cool slightly, then chop. Put the oil, lime juice, water, shallot, peas, chilli and spices in a small pan, bring to the boil, then reduce the heat and simmer gently, stirring

occasionally, for 3 minutes. Stir in the potato, carrot and cauliflower and transfer to a bowl to cool.

2 To make the pastry, sift the flours into a bowl, add the margarine and rub in with your fingertips until the mixture resembles breadcrumbs. Add just enough milk to make a firm dough.

Turn out on to a lightly floured work surface and knead gently until smooth. Divide the dough into 4 equal pieces and roll each out into an 18-cm/7-inch round. Trim the edges and cut each round in half.

3 Brush a baking sheet with a little sunflower oil. Divide the vegetable mixture between the dough

semi-circles, placing it on one half only and leaving a small border. Brush the edges with water, fold the dough over and seal, pressing the edges together. Brush with beaten egg, transfer to the baking sheet and bake in the oven for 20–25 minutes, or until golden brown. Serve hot or cold with mango chutney.

layered vegetable bake

serves 4 **prep: 10 mins** **cook: 1 hr 30 mins**

Simplicity itself, this tasty bake makes a superb meal in itself or can be served as a vegetable accompaniment to griddled chicken, in which case it will serve 8 people.

INGREDIENTS

1 tbsp olive oil, for brushing

675 g/1½ lb potatoes

2 leeks

2 beef tomatoes

8 fresh basil leaves

1 garlic clove, finely chopped

300 ml/10 fl oz Vegetable Stock
(see page 11)

salt and pepper

NUTRITIONAL INFORMATION

Calories 174

Protein 5g

Carbohydrate 33g

Sugars 4g

Fat 4g

Saturates 1g

variation

You could add 2 thinly sliced courgettes to the layers of leeks for an even more substantial supper dish.

1 Preheat the oven to 180°C/350°F/Gas Mark 4. Brush a large ovenproof dish with a little of the olive oil. Prepare all the vegetables. Peel and thinly slice the potatoes, trim and slice the leeks and slice the tomatoes. Place a layer of potato slices in the base of the dish, sprinkle with half the basil leaves and cover with a layer of leeks. Top with a layer of tomato slices. Repeat these layers until all the vegetables are used up, ending with a layer of potatoes.

2 Stir the garlic into the vegetable stock and season to taste with salt and pepper. Pour the stock over the vegetables and brush the top with the remaining olive oil.

3 Bake in the preheated oven for 1½ hours, or until the vegetables are tender and the topping is golden brown. Serve immediately.

cottage potatoes

cook: 1 hr   **prep: 10 mins**   **serves 4**

Give the humble potato a surprising kick with this delicious spiced cheese filling. Serve with a tomato and onion salad or on a bed of colourful mixed salad leaves.

NUTRITIONAL INFORMATION

Calories 211

Protein 11g

Carbohydrate 29g

Sugars 3g

Fat 6g

Saturates 1g

INGREDIENTS

4 baking potatoes

2 tsp sun-dried tomato purée

½ tsp ground coriander

salt and pepper

1 tbsp olive oil

3–4 spring onions, finely chopped

1–2 fresh green chillies, deseeded and finely chopped

1 tbsp tequila

1 tbsp finely chopped fresh coriander

225 g/8 oz low-fat cottage cheese

fresh coriander sprigs, to garnish

lime wedges, to serve

cook's tip

To cook the potatoes in the microwave, prick with a fork and put on kitchen paper. Cook on High for 6 minutes, turn over and cook for a further 8 minutes.

1 Preheat the oven to 200°C/400°F/Gas Mark 6. Cut a cross in the centre of each potato and prick the skins with a fork. Wrap the potatoes individually in foil and bake for 1 hour, or until soft and cooked through.

2 Meanwhile, mix the sun-dried tomato purée and ground coriander together in a small bowl. Season to taste with salt and pepper. Just before the potatoes are ready, heat the olive oil in a small saucepan and add the spring onions and chopped chillies. Cook, stirring occasionally, for 2–3 minutes, or until softened. Stir in the sun-dried tomato paste mixture and tequila and cook for a further 1 minute. Remove from the heat and stir in the chopped coriander. Place the cottage cheese in a bowl and stir in the tomato mixture. Blend thoroughly.

3 Unwrap the potatoes and squeeze gently to open out the cut side. Divide the cottage cheese mixture equally among the potatoes and garnish with coriander. Serve with lime wedges.

falafel

makes 24 **prep: 15 mins, plus 1 hr chilling** **cook: 2 hrs**

These scrumptious Middle Eastern morsels are a must-have on a buffet table and are ideal snacks for any time of day. Traditionally they are deep-fried, but here they are oven-baked and served with a spicy yogurt dip to counteract the slightly drier texture.

NUTRITIONAL INFORMATION

Calories 42

Protein 3g

Carbohydrate 6g

Sugars 1g

Fat 1g

Saturates 0g

INGREDIENTS

225 g/8 oz dried chickpeas, soaked
overnight and drained

1 onion, chopped

2 garlic cloves, chopped

2 tsp cumin seeds

2 tsp ground coriander

2 tbsp chopped fresh parsley

2 tbsp chopped fresh coriander

salt and pepper

sunflower or corn oil, for brushing

DIP

150 ml/5 fl oz low-fat natural yogurt

1 tbsp chopped fresh coriander

1 tbsp chopped fresh mint

2 tsp grated onion

1 fresh red chilli, deseeded and
finely chopped

¼ tsp ground cumin

dash of lemon juice

variation

If time is limited use 225 g/8 oz canned chickpeas instead of the dried. Replace the yogurt with fat-free fromage frais for a thicker dip.

cook's tip

When cooking dried chickpeas, skim off any scum that rises to the surface during cooking with a slotted spoon and always season after they have been cooked, otherwise they will become tough.

1 Put the chickpeas in a saucepan, cover with water and bring to the boil over a medium heat. Cook for 1–1½ hours, or until tender, then drain. Put the chickpeas, onion, garlic, cumin seeds, ground coriander, parsley and fresh coriander in a food processor and process until a firm paste forms. Transfer to a bowl, season to taste with salt and pepper, cover with clingfilm and leave to chill in the refrigerator for 1 hour.

2 To make the dip, mix all the ingredients together in a bowl, cover and chill in the refrigerator until required.

3 Preheat the oven to 200°C/400°F/Gas Mark 6. Brush a baking sheet with sunflower oil. Using your hands, form the chickpea mixture into walnut-sized balls, place on the baking sheet and flatten them slightly. Brush with sunflower oil and bake in the oven for 15 minutes. Turn over and bake for a further 15 minutes, or until brown. Serve warm, with the yogurt dip.

poor man's tomatoes

serves 4 **prep: 20 mins** **cook: 35 mins**

These elegantly filled tomatoes are perfect for any occasion, whether they are used for a family supper or as a starter for a dinner party. They are ideal served with a fresh, crisp salad.

INGREDIENTS

4 large tomatoes

2 tbsp finely chopped fresh basil

4 tsp olive oil

280 g/10 oz button mushrooms, very finely chopped

1 small onion, very finely chopped

2 garlic cloves, very finely chopped

1 tablespoon chopped fresh parsley

salt and pepper

225 ml/8 fl oz Vegetable Stock (see page 11)

1 tbsp freshly grated Parmesan cheese

fresh basil sprigs, to garnish

NUTRITIONAL INFORMATION

Calories	.78
Protein	.3g
Carbohydrate	.6g
Sugars	.6g
Fat	.5g
Saturates	.1g

variation

To fill peppers, cut the tops off and remove the seeds. Blanch in boiling water for 2 minutes. Drain. Make the stuffing with 4 tomatoes.

1 Preheat the oven to 180°C/350°F/Gas Mark 4. Slice a 'lid' from the top of each tomato and reserve. Using a teaspoon, carefully scoop out the flesh from the tomato shells and chop. Place it in a small bowl and add 1 teaspoon of the chopped fresh basil. Invert the tomato shells on kitchen paper to drain.

2 Heat 3 teaspoons of the olive oil in a frying pan. Add the mushrooms, onion, garlic, parsley and remaining basil and season to taste with pepper. Cover and cook over a low heat for 2 minutes, then remove the lid and cook, stirring occasionally, for a further 8–10 minutes. Meanwhile, bring the stock to the boil and cook until reduced by three-quarters. Stir in the tomato mixture and cook for a further 3–4 minutes, or until thickened. Rub the mixture through a sieve with a wooden spoon and stir it into the mushroom mixture. Stir in the Parmesan cheese.

3 Stand the tomatoes, the right way up, in an ovenproof dish and season the insides with salt. Divide the stuffing mixture between them and replace the 'lids'. Brush with the remaining olive oil and bake in the preheated oven for 15 minutes, or until tender and cooked through. Garnish with a few sprigs of fresh basil and serve warm.

corn & pepper pancakes

cook: 20 mins **prep: 15 mins** **serves 4**

These light-as-air pancakes are very moreish, so it's fortunate that they are so easy to make. For best results, use a heavy-based frying pan or griddle pan, preferably one with a non-stick lining.

NUTRITIONAL INFORMATION	
Calories	.239
Protein	.8g
Carbohydrate	.40g
Sugars	.3g
Fat	.6g
Saturates	.1g

INGREDIENTS

150 g/5½ oz frozen sweetcorn
kernels, thawed

4 tbsp cornmeal

4 tbsp plain flour

1 small red pepper, deseeded and
very finely chopped

1 small egg yolk

½ tsp caster sugar

2 egg whites

1 tbsp olive oil

variation

You can use the same quantity of fresh sweetcorn as canned, in which case, you will require 1 large cob.

1 Put half the sweetcorn kernels in a food processor and process until finely chopped. Place the remaining sweetcorn kernels, cornmeal, flour and chopped pepper in a bowl and add the processed sweetcorn. Beat the egg yolk with the sugar in a separate small bowl, then add it to the sweetcorn mixture and stir thoroughly.

2 Beat the egg whites in a spotlessly clean, greasefree bowl until they stand in soft peaks. Gently fold half the egg whites into the sweetcorn mixture, then fold in the remaining egg whites.

3 Heat half the olive oil in a heavy-based frying pan. Drop spoonfuls of the batter into the frying pan,

spacing them well apart, and cook for 3 minutes, or until the undersides are golden brown. Flip over carefully with a spatula and cook the other sides for 3 minutes, or until golden brown. Transfer to a warmed serving plate and keep warm while you cook the remaining pancakes, adding more oil, if necessary. Serve immediately.

mackerel & potato salad

serves 4   **prep: 25 mins,** **plus 6 hrs chilling**   **cook: 10 mins**

Inexpensive and packed with flavour, mackerel is an ideal fish to use in salads. In this recipe, it is combined with nutty new potatoes, apple, watercress and cucumber.

INGREDIENTS

125 g/4½ oz new potatoes, scrubbed and diced

225 g/8 oz mackerel fillets, skinned

1.2 litres/2 pints water

1 bay leaf

1 slice of lemon

1 eating apple, cored and diced

1 shallot, thinly sliced

3 tbsp white wine vinegar

1 tsp sunflower oil

1½ tsp caster sugar

¼ tsp Dijon mustard

salt and pepper

TO SERVE

2 tbsp low-fat natural yogurt

¼ cucumber, thinly sliced

1 tbsp snipped fresh chives

1 bunch of watercress

NUTRITIONAL INFORMATION

Calories 182

Protein 12g

Carbohydrate 11g

Sugars 6g

Fat 10g

Saturates 2g

---

variation

Fresh salmon is very versatile and would work equally well in this dish. Replace the mackerel fillets with the same quantity of salmon fillets.

cook's tip

If new potatoes such as Jersey Royals are not in season, use a waxy, firm-fleshed salad variety, such as Pink Fir Apple or Desirée.

1 Steam the potatoes over a saucepan of simmering water for 10 minutes, or until tender. Meanwhile, using a sharp knife, remove the skin from the mackerel fillets and cut into bite-sized pieces. Bring the water to the boil in a large, shallow saucepan, then reduce the heat so that it is just simmering and add the

mackerel pieces, bay leaf and lemon. Poach for 3 minutes, or until the flesh is opaque. Remove the mackerel from the saucepan with a spatula and transfer to a serving dish.

2 Drain the potatoes well and transfer them to a large bowl. Mix with the apple and shallot, then spoon the mixture over the mackerel.

3 Mix the vinegar, oil sugar and mustard together in a jug, season to taste with salt and pepper and whisk thoroughly. Pour the dressing over the potato mixture. Cover and chill in the refrigerator for up to 6 hours.

4 To serve, spread the yogurt over the salad, then arrange the cucumber

decoratively on top and sprinkle with the fresh chives. Surround the salad with the watercress.

cantaloupe & crab salad

serves 4   **prep: 15 mins**   **cook: 0 mins**

This colourful salad combines delicious fresh crabmeat with flavoursome raw fruit and vegetables and a low-fat dressing – what could be healthier or more delicious?

INGREDIENTS

350 g/12 oz fresh crabmeat

5 tbsp Low-fat Mayonnaise
(see page 12)

50 ml/2 fl oz low-fat natural yogurt

4 tsp extra virgin olive oil

4 tsp lime juice

1 spring onion, finely chopped

4 tsp finely chopped fresh parsley

pinch of cayenne pepper

1 cantaloupe melon

2 radicchio heads,
separated into leaves

fresh parsley sprigs, to garnish

NUTRITIONAL INFORMATION

Calories	.252
Protein	.20g
Carbohydrate	.10g
Sugars	.9g
Fat	.15g
Saturates	.1g

cook's tip

If fresh crab meat is not available, you can use frozen crab meat. Allow the crab to thaw thoroughly before making the salad.

1 Place the crabmeat in a large bowl and pick over it very carefully to remove any remaining shell or cartilage, but try not to break the meat up.

2 Put the low-fat mayonnaise, yogurt, olive oil, lime juice, spring onion, chopped fresh parsley and cayenne pepper into a separate bowl and mix until thoroughly blended. Fold in the crabmeat.

3 Cut the melon in half and remove and discard the seeds. Thinly slice, then cut off the rind with a sharp knife.

4 Arrange the melon slices and radicchio leaves on 4 large serving plates, then arrange the crabmeat mixture on top. Garnish with a few sprigs of fresh parsley and serve.

thai noodle salad

⏱ **cook: 3 mins**   ⏱ **prep: 10 mins, plus 30 mins soaking**   **serves 4**

Thai salads are typically a contrasting mix of colours, textures, aromas and flavours, and are designed to delight the eye as much as they tempt the taste buds.

NUTRITIONAL INFORMATION

Calories	.272
Protein	.16g
Carbohydrate	.45g
Sugars	.6g
Fat	.3g
Saturates	.1g

INGREDIENTS

25 g/1 oz dried wood ears

55 g/2 oz dried Chinese mushrooms

115 g/4 oz cellophane noodles

115 g/4 oz cooked lean minced pork

115 g/4 oz peeled raw prawns

5 fresh red chillies, deseeded and thinly sliced

1 tbsp chopped fresh coriander

3 tbsp Thai fish sauce (nam pla)

3 tbsp lime juice

1 tbsp brown sugar

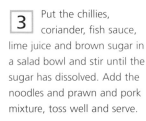

variation

For extra flavour, use the strained soaking water from the mushrooms – not the wood ears – for cooking the prawns and the cooked minced pork.

1 Put the wood ears and Chinese mushrooms in separate bowls and pour over enough boiling water to cover. Leave to soak for 30 minutes. After 20 minutes, put the cellophane noodles in a separate bowl and pour over enough hot water to cover. Leave the noodles to soak for 10 minutes, or according to the packet instructions.

2 Drain the wood ears, rinse thoroughly and cut into small pieces. Drain the mushrooms, squeezing out as much liquid as possible. Cut off and discard the stalks and cut the caps in half. Pour just enough water into a saucepan to cover the base and bring to the boil. Add the pork, prawns, wood ears and mushrooms and simmer, stirring, for 3 minutes,

or until cooked through. Drain well. Drain the noodles and cut them into short lengths with kitchen scissors.

3 Put the chillies, coriander, fish sauce, lime juice and brown sugar in a salad bowl and stir until the sugar has dissolved. Add the noodles and prawn and pork mixture, toss well and serve.

turkey & rice salad

serves 4

prep: 15 mins, ⟳
plus 10 mins cooling

cook: 30 mins ⟳

Rice salads are perfect at any time of year and are both economical and very easy to prepare. To enjoy the delicate flavour of this dish, serve it while it is still warm.

INGREDIENTS

1 litre/1¾ pints Chicken Stock
(see page 11)

175 g/6 oz mixed long-grain
and wild rice

2 tbsp sunflower or corn oil

225 g/8 oz skinless, boneless turkey
breast, trimmed of all visible fat and
cut into thin strips

225 g/8 oz mangetout

115 g/4 oz oyster mushrooms,
torn into pieces

55 g/2 oz shelled pistachio nuts,
finely chopped

2 tbsp chopped fresh coriander

1 tbsp snipped fresh garlic chives

salt and pepper

1 tbsp balsamic vinegar

fresh garlic chives, to garnish

NUTRITIONAL INFORMATION

Calories 373

Protein 22g

Carbohydrate 40g

Sugars 2g

Fat 14g

Saturates 1g

---

variation

This salad would also look spectacular made with red rice. Cook as in the main recipe or follow the packet instructions.

cook's tip

Before adding any of the ingredients to the preheated hot wok, swirl the sunflower oil gently and carefully so that it coats the sides as well as the base of the wok.

1 Reserve 3 tablespoons of the chicken stock and bring the remainder to the boil in a large saucepan. Add the rice and cook for 30 minutes, or until tender. Drain and leave to cool slightly.

2 Meanwhile, heat 1 tablespoon of the oil in a preheated wok or frying pan. Stir-fry the turkey over a

medium heat for 3–4 minutes, or until cooked through. Using a slotted spoon, transfer the turkey to a dish. Add the mangetout and mushrooms to the wok and stir-fry for 1 minute. Add the reserved stock, bring to the boil, then reduce the heat, cover and simmer for 3–4 minutes. Transfer the vegetables to the dish and leave to cool slightly.

3 Thoroughly mix the rice, turkey, mangetout, mushrooms, nuts, coriander and garlic chives together, then season to taste with salt and pepper. Drizzle with the remaining sunflower oil and the vinegar and garnish with fresh garlic chives. Serve warm.

prawn & rice salad

serves 4　　　　　**prep: 10 mins,** ↺
plus 10 mins cooling　　　　　**cook: 35 mins** ⏱

This colourful tropical salad is simplicity itself to prepare and tastes simply wonderful. For a special treat, you could use tiger prawns rather than their smaller Atlantic or Mediterranean cousins.

INGREDIENTS

175 g/6 oz mixed long-grain
and wild rice
salt and pepper
350 g/12 oz cooked peeled prawns
1 mango, peeled, stoned and diced
4 spring onions, sliced
25 g/1 oz flaked almonds
1 tbsp finely chopped fresh mint

DRESSING
1 tbsp extra virgin olive oil
2 tsp lime juice
1 garlic clove, crushed
1 tsp clear honey
salt and pepper

NUTRITIONAL INFORMATION

Calories 345

Protein 25g

Carbohydrate 43g

Sugars 8g

Fat 8g

Saturates 1g

variation

Substitute the same quantity of fresh or drained canned crabmeat for the prawns, if you like.

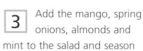

cook's tip

If using tiger prawns for this dish instead of the ordinary ones, buy already cooked and peeled prawns, which are available from most large supermarkets.

1 Cook the rice in a large saucepan of lightly salted boiling water for 35 minutes, or until tender. Drain and transfer to a large bowl, then add the prawns.

2 To make the dressing, mix all the ingredients together in a large jug, seasoning to taste with the salt and pepper, and whisk well until thoroughly blended. Pour the dressing over the rice and prawn mixture and leave to cool.

3 Add the mango, spring onions, almonds and mint to the salad and season to taste with pepper. Stir thoroughly and transfer to a large serving dish and serve.

sweet potato & bean salad

serves 4 **prep: 10 mins** **cook: 10 mins**

This piquant vegetarian salad is a meal in itself or can be served as an accompaniment to chicken or fish. Choose a mixture of colourful salad leaves with a range of sweet and bitter flavours.

INGREDIENTS

1 sweet potato

4 baby carrots, halved

4 tomatoes

4 celery sticks, chopped

225 g/8 oz canned borlotti beans, drained and rinsed

115 g/4 oz mixed salad leaves, such as frisée, rocket, radicchio and oakleaf lettuce

1 tbsp sultanas

4 spring onions, finely chopped

125 ml/4 fl oz Honey and Yogurt Dressing (see Cook's Tip, page 12)

NUTRITIONAL INFORMATION

Calories 143

Protein 6g

Carbohydrate 29g

Sugars 22g

Fat 1g

Saturates 1g

variation

Substitute your favourite beans for the borlotti beans – cannellini or flageolets would be equally good.

cook's tip

Cook the sweet potato in boiling water until it is just tender, otherwise it will absorb too much water and become unpleasantly soggy.

1 Peel and dice the sweet potato. Bring a saucepan of water to the boil over a medium heat. Add the sweet potato and cook for 10 minutes, until tender. Drain the potato, transfer to a bowl and set aside.

2 Cook the carrots in a separate saucepan of boiling water for 1 minute.

Drain thoroughly and add to the sweet potato. Cut the tops off the tomatoes and scoop out the seeds. Chop the flesh and add to the bowl with the celery and beans. Mix well.

3 Line a large serving bowl with the mixed salad leaves. Spoon the sweet potato and bean mixture on top, then sprinkle with the

sultanas and spring onions. Spoon over the dressing and serve immediately.

main dishes

This chapter is the answer to that perennial question – what shall we have for
supper tonight? Finding a solution can be a real headache when every cookbook you turn to
for good ideas seems packed with recipes notable for their heavy use of butter, cream and other
high-fat ingredients. Inspired by cuisines around the world, from Greece to China and from
Morocco to Germany, these recipes feature marvellous main dishes based on meat,
poultry and vegetables. Many of them contain no more than 15 g (½ oz) fat per
serving and some contain far less.

Stun sceptical guests with Stuffed Pork Fillet (see page 88), Roast Turkey with
Cider Sauce (see page 108) or Moroccan Vegetable Stew (see page 112). No one will ever
suggest again that low-fat cooking is boring and bland. Seduce the family into a healthier
lifestyle with Swedish Lamb Stew (see page 98), Chicken with Saffron Mash (see page 100)
or Vegetable & Tofu Stir-fry (see page 110). Roasts, casseroles, stews, grills and stir-fries
are just some of the mouthwatering, healthy options that spoil you for choice. There is
a dish for every season and all tastes, from subtle and creamy to warm and spicy.
You will find quick and easy recipes for midweek suppers, succulent slow-cooked dishes
for restful weekends and gourmet delights for low-fat entertaining.

beef & broccoli in black bean sauce

serves 4　　　　　**prep: 10 mins,** ⏼ **plus 6 hrs marinating**　　　　　**cook: 15 mins** ⏱

Stir-fries are not only quick and easy to cook, but a healthy choice as well. Because the cooking time is so brief, the vegetables retain most of their nutrients – and their flavour and texture too.

INGREDIENTS

225 g/8 oz lean rump steak

1 tbsp peanut or corn oil

225 g/8 oz broccoli, cut into florets

115 g/4 oz baby corn cobs, cut in half diagonally

3 tbsp water

4 spring onions, sliced diagonally

225 g/8 oz canned water chestnuts, drained, rinsed and sliced

MARINADE

1 tbsp fermented black beans, soaked in cold water for 5–10 minutes

2 tbsp dark soy sauce

2 tbsp Chinese rice vinegar

1 tbsp peanut or corn oil

1 tsp brown sugar

1 garlic clove, thinly sliced

1 tbsp finely chopped fresh root ginger

NUTRITIONAL INFORMATION

Calories 190

Protein 16g

Carbohydrates 12g

Sugars 3g

Fat 9g

Saturates 2g

variation

Use different combinations of vegetables for this stir-fry, such as courgette strips, carrot matchsticks, pepper strips and cucumber batons.

cook's tip

Fermented black beans are available in cans or bags from Chinese food shops. They should be soaked in cold water before use to remove any excess salt.

1 Using a sharp knife, trim the steak of all visible fat and thinly slice. Put the steak in a shallow, non-metallic dish. To make the marinade, mash the black beans in a bowl with a fork. Stir in the remaining ingredients until thoroughly blended. Pour the marinade over the steak, turning to coat thoroughly. Cover with clingfilm and leave in the refrigerator to marinate for up to 6 hours.

2 Heat the peanut oil in a preheated wok or large frying pan. Drain the steak and reserve the marinade. Stir-fry the steak over a medium–high heat for 3 minutes, then transfer to a plate. Add the broccoli and baby corn cobs to the wok and stir in the water. Cover and steam over a low heat for 5 minutes, or until the vegetables are tender.

3 Add the spring onions and water chestnuts to the wok. Stir-fry for 2 minutes. Return the steak to the wok and pour in the reserved marinade. Cook, stirring, until heated through, then serve.

meatballs with tomato relish

serves 4   **prep: 15 mins**   **cook: 15–20 mins**

Even when minced beef is labelled 'lean', it may contain more fat than we would like. It is best to buy a whole piece of lean beef, such as rump steak, trim off all visible fat and mince it yourself.

INGREDIENTS

1 onion, finely chopped

2 garlic cloves, finely chopped

2 slices bread, crusts removed

500 g/1 lb 2 oz lean beef, minced

1 cooked baby beetroot, chopped

pinch of paprika

2 tsp finely chopped fresh thyme

1 egg

salt and pepper

fresh thyme sprigs, to garnish

TOMATO RELISH

150 ml/5 fl oz passata

2 tsp creamed horseradish

NUTRITIONAL INFORMATION

Calories	243
Protein	30g
Carbohydrate	14g
Sugars	5g
Fat	8g
Saturates	3g

cook's tip

It is easy to cook beetroot yourself. Clean them and trim the stalks, then cook in a saucepan of simmering lightly salted water for 1–2 hours until tender. Drain and cool, then peel.

1 Preheat the oven to 230°C/450°F/Gas Mark 8. To make the tomato relish, mix the passata and creamed horseradish together in a small bowl. Cover and set aside until required.

2 Put the onion, garlic and 2 teaspoons of water in a small saucepan and simmer over a low heat for 5 minutes. Increase the heat, bring to the boil and cook until all the water has evaporated. Remove from the heat.

3 Meanwhile, tear the bread into pieces and place in a small bowl. Add enough cold water just to cover and leave to soak for 5 minutes. Squeeze the excess water from the bread and place in a bowl with the minced beef, onion and garlic mixture, beetroot, paprika, thyme and egg. Season to taste with salt and pepper and mix thoroughly.

4 Form the mixture into 24 small balls between the palms of your hands. Thread 3 balls onto each of 8 skewers and place on a baking sheet. Bake in the preheated oven for 10 minutes, or until well browned. Transfer to a serving dish, garnish with a few sprigs of fresh thyme and serve with the tomato relish.

beef in beer

⏱ **cook: 2 hrs–2 hrs 30 mins**   🕐 **prep: 15 mins**   **serves 4**

Beef and beer is a traditional combination in all brewing countries, especially in Belgium, Germany and Ireland. Use a strong dark beer or stout to create the fullest flavour.

NUTRITIONAL INFORMATION

Calories	.224
Protein	.27g
Carbohydrate	.6g
Sugars	.5g
Fat	.9g
Saturates	.3g

INGREDIENTS

few sprigs of fresh parsley

1 tbsp sunflower or corn oil

500 g/1 lb 2 oz lean stewing steak, trimmed of all visible fat and cut into 2.5-cm/1-inch cubes

1 onion, chopped

200 g/7 oz chestnut mushrooms, cut in half

4 tsp dark muscovado sugar

350 ml/12 fl oz Beef Stock (see page 11)

300 ml/10 fl oz dark beer or stout

salt and pepper

variation

You could add 1 thinly sliced carrot and 2 thinly sliced celery sticks halfway through cooking the mushrooms in Step 2.

1 Using a sharp knife, chop the fresh parsley finely and set aside until required. Heat the sunflower oil in a large, heavy-based frying pan. Add the stewing steak and cook, stirring frequently, for 10 minutes, or until browned all over. Using a slotted spoon, transfer the meat to a large flameproof casserole dish.

2 Add the onion to the frying pan and cook over a low heat, stirring occasionally, for 3 minutes. Add the mushrooms and sugar and cook, stirring occasionally, for 10 minutes. Transfer to the casserole with a slotted spoon.

3 Add the beef stock, beer and reserved parsley to the casserole and season to taste with salt and pepper. Bring to the boil, cover and simmer over a very low heat for 1½–2 hours, or until tender. Serve hot.

sauerbraten

serves 4

**prep: 20 mins,
plus 48 hrs marinating**

cook: 2 hrs 15 mins

In this traditional German dish, long marinating makes the topside melt-in-the-mouth tender and imparts a marvellous spicy flavour. This dish makes the perfect treat for a special occasion.

INGREDIENTS

750 g/1 lb 10 oz topside of beef, trimmed of all visible fat

8 whole cloves

1 tbsp sunflower or corn oil

225 ml/8 fl oz Beef Stock (see page 11)

1 kg/2 lb 4 oz mixed root vegetables, such as carrots, potatoes and swede, peeled and cut into large chunks

2 tbsp raisins

1½ tsp cornflour

3 tbsp water

salt and pepper

MARINADE

200 ml/7 fl oz wine

5 tbsp red wine vinegar

1 onion, chopped

1½ tsp brown sugar

4 peppercorns

1 bay leaf

½ tsp ground mixed spice

½ tsp mustard

NUTRITIONAL INFORMATION

Calories	.445
Protein	.41g
Carbohydrate	.36g
Sugars	.25g
Fat	.12g
Saturates	.4g

variation

Try other root vegetables with this dish, such as chunks of parsnip, turnip and celeriac.

cook's tip

This rustic dish will taste superb if you serve it with a simple and traditional accompaniment of boiled potatoes or noodles.

1 To make the marinade, put all the ingredients, except the mustard, in a saucepan. Bring to simmering point, then remove from the heat and stir in the mustard. Stud the beef with cloves and place in a non-metallic dish. Pour the marinade over, cover and leave to cool, then chill in the refrigerator for 2 days. About 1 hour before cooking,

remove the beef, pat dry and stand at room temperature. Reserve the marinade.

2 Preheat the oven to 150°C/300°F/ Gas Mark 2. Heat the oil in a flameproof casserole, add the beef and cook over a medium heat for 5–10 minutes, or until browned. Pour the marinade into the casserole through a

sieve, add the stock and bring to the boil. Cover and bake in the oven for 1 hour, turning and basting frequently with the cooking juices.

3 Meanwhile, blanch the vegetables in boiling water for 3 minutes, then drain. Arrange the vegetables around the beef, return to the oven and cook for 1 hour, or

until the beef is very tender and the vegetables are cooked.

4 Transfer the beef and vegetables to a serving dish. Place the casserole on a low heat and add the raisins. Mix the cornflour and water until smooth and stir into the cooking juices. Bring to the boil, stirring, then simmer for 2–3 minutes. Season and serve.

stuffed pork fillet

serves 8   **prep: 25 mins, plus 6 hrs chilling (optional)**   **cook: 1 hr 30 mins**

Dried fruit, such as prunes and apricots, balances the richness of pork superbly. This succulent pork fillet is perfect served hot for a family supper and would also be an excellent choice, served cold, for a buffet, summer party or picnic.

INGREDIENTS

2 pork fillets, about 500 g/1 lb 2 oz each, trimmed of all visible fat

STUFFING

2 red onions, finely chopped

115 g/4 oz fresh wholemeal breadcrumbs

85 g/3 oz no-soak dried prunes, chopped

85 g/3 oz no-soak dried apricots, chopped

pinch of grated nutmeg

pinch of ground cinnamon

salt and pepper

1 egg white, lightly beaten

variation

For an elegant presentation, garnish the pork fillet with fresh watercress and serve, adding a few watercress leaves to each plate.

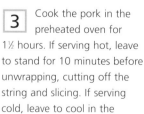

cook's tip

Dried fruit that does not need soaking is often labelled as 'ready-to-eat' fruit, and is available in the baking section of most large supermarkets.

1 Preheat the oven to 200°C/400°F/Gas Mark 6. To make the stuffing, mix the onions, breadcrumbs, prunes and apricots together. Season to taste with nutmeg, cinnamon, and salt and pepper. Stir in the egg white.

2 Cut a 13-cm/5-inch long piece from the narrow end of each pork fillet, then cut all the pieces almost completely in half lengthways and open them out. Spread half the filling evenly over one of the longer pieces, then cover with both the smaller pieces, overlapping the narrow ends slightly. Spread the remaining filling on top and cover with the remaining piece of pork. Tie the pork loaf together with kitchen string or trussing thread at intervals along its length. Wrap it securely in foil and place in a roasting tin.

3 Cook the pork in the preheated oven for 1½ hours. If serving hot, leave to stand for 10 minutes before unwrapping, cutting off the string and slicing. If serving cold, leave to cool in the wrapping, then leave to chill in the refrigerator for at least 2 hours and up to 6 hours before unwrapping and slicing.

stir-fried pork with mangetout

serves 4 **prep: 25 mins, plus 6 hrs chilling (optional)** **cook: 20 mins**

Served with rice or noodles, this substantial stir-fry makes a delicious midweek family supper. Prepare the garnish before you begin cooking and serve with a flourish.

INGREDIENTS

8 dried Chinese mushrooms

450 g/1 lb pork fillet, trimmed of all visible fat and cut into thin strips

115 g/4 oz baby corn cobs

1 tbsp groundnut or corn oil

1 garlic clove, finely chopped

2.5-cm/1-inch piece fresh root ginger, cut into thin batons

400 g/14 oz mangetout

400 g/14 oz canned bamboo shoots, drained, rinsed and thinly sliced

2 tsp dark soy sauce

2 tsp Chinese rice wine

4 tbsp Chicken or Vegetable Stock (see page 11)

2 tsp cornflour

2 tbsp water

1 carrot, sliced into thin batons

salt and pepper

1–2 spring onions, trimmed, to garnish

MARINADE

1 tbsp dark soy sauce

1 tbsp Chinese rice wine

2 tsp cornflour

pepper

variation

You could add an extra, thinly sliced carrot and 2 thinly sliced celery sticks halfway through cooking the mushrooms in step 4, if you like.

cook's tip

To rehydrate Chinese dried mushrooms, place the mushrooms in a small bowl and pour over enough hot water to cover. Leave to soak for 20 minutes.

1 To make the garnish, make a lengthways cut 2.5-cm/1-inch long at one end of each spring onion. Roll the onion through 90° and repeat. Repeat at the other end, then place in iced water to open out. Pat dry before using.

2 Rehydrate the Chinese mushrooms (see Cook's Tip). Mix all the marinade ingredients together in a non-metallic dish, seasoning with the pepper. Add the pork, cover and chill for 20 minutes. Blanch the corn in boiling water for 5 minutes. Drain and refresh in cold water.

3 Drain the mushrooms through a sieve, reserving the soaking water. Squeeze out any excess water, remove the stems and slice the caps. Heat half the oil in a preheated wok, add the pork and stir-fry for 5 minutes, until browned. Remove and reserve.

4 Wipe the wok, add the remaining oil and heat. Add the garlic and cook until golden. Remove with a slotted spoon and discard. Add the ginger, mangetout, bamboo shoots and mushrooms and stir-fry for 3 minutes. Stir in the soy sauce, wine, stock and reserved soaking liquid. Cook for 2–3 minutes. Mix the cornflour and water, add to the wok and stir until thickened. Return the pork and cooking juices to the wok, add the corn and cook until heated through. Stir in the carrot, garnish with spring onion tassels and serve.

char shiu pork

serves 4   **prep: 20 mins, plus 2 hrs marinating**   **cook: 15–20 mins**

The aromatic star anise gives this very famous traditional Cantonese dish its characteristic flavour, while the dark soy sauce is the secret of the rich and appetising colour.

INGREDIENTS

600 g/1 lb 5 oz pork fillet, trimmed of all visible fat

2 tbsp dark soy sauce

2 spring onions, finely chopped

2.5-cm/1-inch piece fresh root ginger, finely chopped

1 tsp red fermented bean curd

2 star anise

1 tbsp Chinese rice wine

1 tbsp clear honey

1½ tsp Chinese rice vinegar

½ tsp cornflour

1 tbsp water

NUTRITIONAL INFORMATION

Calories	.260
Protein	.32g
Carbohydrate	.9g
Sugars	.5g
Fat	.11g
Saturates	.4g

cook's tip

Char shui pork can also be cooked on a barbecue. Cook for 15 minutes over hot coals, turning and brushing frequently with the honey glaze.

1 Brush the pork all over with half the soy sauce and leave to stand for 15 minutes. Meanwhile, place the spring onions, ginger, bean curd and star anise in a mortar and pound to a paste with a pestle. Transfer to a shallow, non-metallic dish and stir in the Chinese rice wine, half the honey, 1 teaspoon of the vinegar and the remaining soy sauce. Add the pork, turning to coat. Cover and leave in the refrigerator to marinate for 2 hours, turning the pork every 20 minutes.

2 Preheat the oven to 220°C/425°F/Gas Mark 7. Remove the pork from the marinade and pat dry with kitchen paper. Reserve the marinade. Mix the remaining honey and vinegar with 1 teaspoon of hot water in a small bowl and brush the glaze all over the pork. Place the pork on a rack in a roasting tin and roast in the oven for 10–12 minutes, or until the juices run clear when the meat is pierced with a skewer. Turn the pork once during cooking and brush with the remaining honey glaze.

3 Remove the pork from the oven, cover with foil and leave to stand for 10 minutes. Meanwhile, bring the reserved marinade to the boil in a saucepan. Mix the cornflour and water until smooth, add to the marinade and stir until thickened. Cut the pork across the grain into 5-mm/¼-inch slices. Serve with the marinade for dipping.

griddled pork with orange sauce

⏱ **cook: 10 mins**   ⏱ **prep: 10 mins, plus 3 hrs marinating**   **serves 4**

In this recipe, the pork is garnished with gremolata, a popular Italian seasoning mixture with a citrus tang, which gives the dish a refreshing summery flavour.

NUTRITIONAL INFORMATION

Calories	204
Protein	. . . . .26g
Carbohydrate	. . . . .2g
Sugars	. . . . .1g
Fat	. . . . .10g
Saturates	. . . . .3g

INGREDIENTS

4 tbsp freshly squeezed orange juice

4 tbsp red wine vinegar

2 garlic cloves, finely chopped

pepper

4 pork steaks, trimmed of all visible fat

olive oil, for brushing

GREMOLATA

3 tbsp finely chopped fresh parsley

grated rind of 1 lime

grated rind of ½ lemon

1 garlic clove, very finely chopped

variation

This dish would work equally well with chicken breast portions. Remove the skin from the cooked chicken before serving.

1 Mix the orange juice, vinegar and garlic together in a shallow, non-metallic dish and season to taste with pepper. Add the pork, turning to coat. Cover and leave in the refrigerator to marinate for up to 3 hours.

2 Meanwhile, mix all the gremolata ingredients together in a small mixing bowl, cover with clingfilm and leave to chill in the refrigerator until required.

3 Heat a non-stick griddle pan and brush lightly with olive oil. Remove the pork from the marinade, reserving the marinade, add to the pan and cook over a medium–high heat for 5 minutes on each side, or until the juices run clear when the meat is pierced with a skewer.

4 Meanwhile, pour the marinade into a small saucepan and simmer over a medium heat for 5 minutes, or until slightly thickened. Transfer the pork to a serving dish, pour the orange sauce over it and sprinkle with the gremolata. Serve immediately.

lamb tagine

serves 4   **prep: 10 mins**   **cook: 1 hr 40 mins**

This is a typical Moroccan mixture of meat, vegetables and apricots, flavoured with plenty of fresh herbs and spices. It is delicious – and authentic – if served with couscous, which can be cooked in a steamer set over the stew for 6–7 mins.

INGREDIENTS

1 tbsp sunflower or corn oil

1 onion, chopped

350 g/12 oz boneless lamb, trimmed of all visible fat and cut into 2.5-cm/1-inch cubes

1 garlic clove, finely chopped

600 ml/1 pint Vegetable Stock (see page 11)

grated rind and juice of 1 orange

1 tsp clear honey

1 cinnamon stick

1-cm/½-inch piece fresh root ginger, finely chopped

1 aubergine

4 tomatoes, peeled and chopped

115 g/4 oz no-soak dried apricots

2 tbsp chopped fresh coriander

salt and pepper

freshly cooked couscous, to serve

NUTRITIONAL INFORMATION

Calories 267

Protein 21g

Carbohydrate 22g

Sugars 21g

Fat 11g

Saturates 4g

variation

This stew can also be made with the same quantity of no-soak prunes. Alternatively, add 55 g/2 oz no-soak apricots and 55 g/2 oz raisins.

cook's tip

Large aubergines benefit from being sprinkled with salt and left to stand for 30 minutes to remove the bitter juices. Smaller aubergines can be used without salting.

1 Heat the sunflower oil in a large, heavy-based frying pan or flameproof casserole. Add the onion and lamb cubes and cook over a medium heat, stirring frequently, for 5 minutes, or until the meat is lightly browned all over. Add the garlic, vegetable stock, orange rind and juice, honey, cinnamon stick and ginger.

Bring to the boil, then reduce the heat, cover and simmer for 45 minutes.

2 Using a sharp knife, halve the aubergine lengthways and slice thinly. Add to the frying pan with the chopped tomatoes and apricots. Cover and cook for a further 45 minutes, or until the lamb is tender.

3 Stir in the coriander, season to taste with salt and pepper and serve immediately, straight from the frying pan, with the freshly cooked couscous.

greek lamb parcel

serves 4   **prep: 25 mins,**  **plus 8 hrs marinating**   **cook: 35 mins**

Steaming is an excellent low-fat cooking technique. It is essential that the steamer has a tight-fitting lid. If it doesn't, wrap a clean tea towel around the lid to ensure it fits snugly.

INGREDIENTS

500 g/1 lb 2 oz boneless lamb, trimmed of all visible fat and cut into small cubes

2 tsp olive oil

1 red pepper, deseeded and finely chopped

4 tomatoes, peeled and roughly chopped

1 aubergine, roughly chopped

1 courgette, roughly chopped

4 shallots, cut into wedges

salt and pepper

1 tbsp chopped fresh mint

1 tbsp snipped fresh chives

100 ml/3½ fl oz Vegetable Stock (see page 11)

150 ml/5 fl oz low-fat natural yogurt

fresh rosemary sprigs, to garnish

MARINADE

4 tsp mavrodaphne or sweet sherry

1 shallot, finely chopped

1 garlic clove, finely chopped

1 tsp olive oil

salt and pepper

NUTRITIONAL INFORMATION

Calories	.310
Protein	.30g
Carbohydrate	.12g
Sugars	.11g
Fat	.14g
Saturates	.6g

variation

Boneless leg of lamb is also ideal for this dish. If shallots are unavailable, replace with 1 sliced onion.

cook's tip

During the marinating process, turn the meat occasionally with a slotted spoon. Before cooking, drain the meat thoroughly and bring it to room temperature.

1 Place the lamb in a non-metallic dish. Mix all the marinade ingredients together in a bowl, seasoning to taste. Pour the marinade over the lamb, turning to coat well. Cover and leave in the refrigerator to marinate for 8 hours, or overnight. Remove from the marinade and pat dry with kitchen paper. Reserve the marinade.

2 Heat the olive oil in a heavy-based frying pan. Add the lamb and cook, stirring, for 5 minutes, or until browned. Stir in the pepper, tomatoes, aubergine, courgette and shallots and season to taste. Cut a piece of foil large enough to contain the lamb mixture and spoon the mixture onto it, sprinkle with half the mint and half the

chives and turn up the edges of the foil. Return the pan to the heat, add the stock and bring to the boil, scraping up any sediment on the base. Boil until thickened, then pour over the lamb. Seal the foil parcel and place in a steamer set over a saucepan of boiling water. Cover and steam for 30 minutes, topping up with more water, if necessary.

3 Meanwhile, bring the marinade to the boil in a saucepan. Stir in the remaining mint and chives, then remove from the heat and cool. Transfer the lamb mixture to a warmed dish. Stir the yogurt into the marinade and pour over the lamb. Garnish with rosemary sprigs and serve.

swedish lamb stew

serves 4 **prep: 15 mins** **cook: 2 hrs**

This hearty, dill-flavoured lamb stew is a welcome sight on a cold winter evening. Serve with steamed vegetables and plenty of crusty bread to mop up the delicious juices, if you like.

INGREDIENTS

450 g/1 lb boneless lamb

salt and white pepper

1 onion, cut into wedges

2 fresh dill sprigs

1 bay leaf

6 green peppercorns

1 fennel bulb, thinly sliced

115 g/4 oz puffball mushrooms

2 tsp cornflour

1 tbsp skimmed milk

grated rind and juice of ½ lemon

150 ml/5 fl oz Greek-style yogurt

1 tsp mild mustard

4 tbsp snipped fresh dill

NUTRITIONAL INFORMATION

Calories 276

Protein 28g

Carbohydrate 11g

Sugars 5g

Fat 14g

Saturates 7g

variation

If you prefer, you can substitute whole button mushrooms for the puffball mushrooms.

cook's tip

If you have more cooking liquid than you require in Step 2, cool and freeze the excess to use in another lamb dish. As lamb stock is strongly flavoured, do not use it with other types of meat or poultry.

1 Using a sharp knife, trim off all visible fat from the lamb and cut into 2.5-cm/1-inch cubes. Place the lamb in a large saucepan and cover with cold water. Add a pinch of salt. Bring to the boil over a medium heat and, using a slotted spoon, skim off any scum that rises to the surface. Add the onion, dill sprigs, bay leaf and peppercorns. Reduce

the heat, cover and simmer for 45 minutes. Add the fennel and mushrooms, cover and simmer for 30 minutes, or until the lamb is very tender.

2 Using a slotted spoon, transfer the lamb, onion, fennel and mushrooms to a dish and keep warm. Sieve the cooking liquid and reserve 300 ml/10 fl oz. Rinse the pan,

pour in the reserved cooking liquid and bring to the boil. Mix the cornflour and milk until smooth and stir into the sauce. Reduce the heat and simmer, stirring, for 5 minutes, or until thickened. Stir in the lemon rind and juice.

3 Return the lamb, onion, fennel and mushrooms to the saucepan

and simmer, uncovered, for 5 minutes. Meanwhile, mix the yogurt, mustard and snipped fresh dill together in a small bowl and season to taste with salt and pepper. Stir the yogurt mixture into the stew, transfer to a warmed serving dish and serve immediately.

chicken with saffron mash

serves 4   **prep: 20 mins**   **cook: 25 mins**

The addition of fresh thyme, coriander and lemon juice complements the griddled chicken and saffron mash to perfection. Serve with freshly cooked steamed vegetables, such as carrots, broccoli and French beans, if you like.

INGREDIENTS

550 g/1 lb 4 oz floury potatoes, cut into chunks

1 garlic clove, peeled

1 tsp saffron threads, crushed

1.2 litres/2 pints Chicken or Vegetable Stock (see page 11)

4 skinless, boneless chicken breasts, trimmed of all visible fat

2 tbsp olive oil

1 tbsp lemon juice

1 tbsp chopped fresh thyme

1 tbsp chopped fresh coriander

1 tbsp coriander seeds, crushed

100 ml/3½ fl oz hot skimmed milk

salt and pepper

fresh thyme sprigs, to garnish

NUTRITIONAL INFORMATION

Calories	.310
Protein	.31g
Carbohydrate	.25g
Sugars	.2g
Fat	.10g
Saturates	.2g

variation

Serve sweet potato cream instead. Bake 550 g/1 lb 4 oz sweet potatoes for 1 hour. Scoop out the flesh and mash. Heat and stir in a little butter.

cook's tip

Reserve the stock when you drain the potatoes. Re-heat, stirring in 1 tablespoon of chopped fresh thyme and salt and pepper to taste, then serve as a soup.

1 Put the potatoes, garlic and saffron in a large heavy-based saucepan, add the stock and bring to the boil. Cover and simmer for 20 minutes, or until tender.

2 Meanwhile, brush the chicken breasts all over with half the olive oil and all of the lemon juice. Sprinkle with the fresh thyme and coriander

and crushed coriander seeds. Heat a griddle pan, add the chicken and cook over a medium–high heat for 5 minutes on each side, or until the juices run clear when the meat is pierced with a skewer or the point of a knife. Alternatively, cook the chicken breasts under a preheated grill for 5 minutes on each side.

3 Drain the potatoes and return the contents of the sieve to the saucepan. Add the remaining olive oil and the milk, season to taste with salt and pepper and mash until smooth. Divide the saffron mash between 4 large, warmed serving plates, top with a piece of chicken and garnish with a few sprigs of fresh thyme. Serve.

pan-fried chicken & coriander

serves 4　　　　　　**prep: 15 mins**　　　　　　**cook: 15 mins**

It is difficult to believe that the rich-tasting sauce coating this flavoursome chicken doesn't contain lashings of double cream. Nevertheless, this is a low-fat dish and all it needs as an accompaniment is a steamed green vegetable or a crisp salad.

INGREDIENTS

1 bunch of fresh coriander

1 tbsp sunflower or corn oil

4 skinless, boneless chicken breasts, about 115 g/4 oz each, trimmed of all visible fat

1 tsp cornflour

1 tbsp water

85 ml/3 fl oz low-fat natural yogurt

2 tbsp reduced-fat single cream

175 ml/6 fl oz Chicken Stock (see page 11)

2 tbsp lime juice

2 garlic cloves, finely chopped

1 shallot, finely chopped

1 tomato, peeled, deseeded and chopped

salt and pepper

NUTRITIONAL INFORMATION

Calories 200

Protein 27g

Carbohydrate 6g

Sugars 3g

Fat 8g

Saturates 3g

variation

Instead of fresh coriander, try using fresh tarragon. As tarragon is strongly flavoured, only use a few stems, otherwise it may overpower the dish.

cook's tip

Wrap the chicken portions in pieces of foil to keep warm and to prevent them from drying out after cooking. Before serving, remove from the foil and transfer to plates.

1 Reserve a few coriander sprigs for a garnish and roughly chop the remainder. Heat the sunflower oil in a heavy-based frying pan, add the chicken and cook over a medium heat for 5 minutes on each side, or until the juices run clear when the meat is pierced with a skewer or the point of a knife. Remove from the frying pan and keep warm.

2 Mix the cornflour and water until smooth. Stir in the yogurt and cream. Pour the chicken stock and lime juice into the frying pan and add the garlic and shallot. Reduce the heat and simmer for 1 minute. Stir the tomato into the yogurt mixture and stir the mixture into the frying pan. Season to taste with salt and pepper. Cook, stirring constantly, for 1–2 minutes, or until slightly thickened, but do not let the mixture boil. Stir in the chopped fresh coriander.

3 Place the chicken on a large serving plate, pour the sauce over it and garnish with the reserved coriander sprigs. Serve.

chicken with mustard

The combination of chicken and a mustard and orange sauce is quite irresistible. Cooking the dish is simplicity itself – and, as an extra benefit, so is clearing up afterwards.

INGREDIENTS

1 tbsp sunflower or corn oil

4 skinless, boneless chicken breasts, about 140 g/5 oz each, all visible fat removed

salt and pepper

2 large oranges, peeled and cut into segments, juice reserved (see Cook's Tip)

2 tsp cornflour

150 ml/5 fl oz low-fat natural yogurt

1 tsp wholegrain mustard

fresh parsley sprigs, to garnish

NUTRITIONAL INFORMATION

Calories 267

Protein 34g

Carbohydrate 16g

Sugars 12g

Fat 8g

Saturates 2g

---

variation

Omit the oranges and make the sauce with 2 tablespoons of lemon juice and 1 teaspoon of Dijon mustard instead of the wholegrain.

cook's tip

Use a sharp knife to peel the oranges and make sure that you remove all the pith. Hold the oranges over a bowl to catch the juices and cut down between the membranes to separate into segments.

1 Heat the oil in a large, heavy-based frying pan. Add the chicken breasts and cook over a medium–high heat for 5 minutes on each side, or until tender and the juices run clear when the meat is pierced with a skewer or the point of a knife. Season with a little salt and pepper, remove the chicken from the frying pan, cover with foil and keep warm.

2 Pour the orange juice into a small bowl and stir in the cornflour to make a smooth paste. Stir in the yogurt and mustard, then pour into the frying pan and bring to the boil over a low heat, stirring constantly.

3 Add the orange segments to the frying pan and season to taste with salt and pepper. Stir in any juices that have collected from the chicken. Spoon the sauce onto 4 large, warmed serving plates and top with the chicken. Garnish with parsley sprigs and serve immediately.

chicken fricassée

serves 4　　　　**prep: 15 mins**　　　　**cook: 35–40 mins**

While it is typically cooked in cream, the term fricassée merely denotes cooking the meat – or sometimes fish – in a white sauce, without browning it. Serve with plain boiled rice or new potatoes for a filling supper.

INGREDIENTS

1 tbsp plain flour	225 ml/8 fl oz Chicken Stock
salt and white pepper	(see page 11)
4 skinless, boneless chicken	2 carrots, diced
breasts, about 140 g/5 oz each,	2 celery sticks, diced
trimmed of all visible fat and	225 g/8 oz frozen peas
cut into 2-cm/¾-inch cubes	1 yellow pepper, deseeded and diced
1 tbsp sunflower or corn oil	115 g/4 oz button mushrooms, sliced
8 baby onions	125 ml/4 fl oz low-fat natural yogurt
2 garlic cloves, crushed	3 tbsp chopped fresh parsley

variation

You can substitute skimmed milk for the yogurt and add extra flavour with 1 teaspoon of lemon juice and a pinch of freshly grated nutmeg in Step 3.

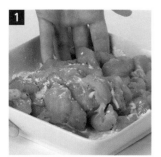

cook's tip

When slicing or dicing pepper halves, place them on a chopping board, shiny side downwards, to prevent the knife from slipping.

1 Spread out the flour on a plate and season with salt and pepper. Add the chicken and, using your hands, coat in the flour. Heat the oil in a heavy-based frying pan. Add the onions and garlic and cook over a low heat, stirring occasionally, for 5 minutes. Add the chicken and cook, stirring, for 10 minutes, or until just beginning to colour.

2 Gradually stir in the chicken stock, then add the carrots, celery and peas. Bring to the boil, then reduce the heat, cover and simmer for 5 minutes. Add the pepper and mushrooms, cover and simmer for a further 10 minutes.

3 Stir in the yogurt and chopped parsley and season to taste with salt and pepper. Cook for 1–2 minutes, or until heated through, then transfer to 4 large, warmed serving plates and serve.

roast turkey with cider sauce

serves 8　　　　　　**prep: 15 mins,**　　　　　**cook: 1 hr 40 mins**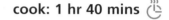
plus 10 mins cooling

Most supermarkets sell boneless turkey breast roast. There is no waste, so it is an economical choice when entertaining and it fits into the oven more easily than a whole bird. Rolling the turkey around the stuffing helps to keep it moist during cooking.

INGREDIENTS

1 kg/1 lb 4 oz boneless turkey
breast roast

salt and pepper

1 tbsp sunflower or corn oil

115 g/4 oz prunes, stoned and chopped

55 g/2 oz raisins

3 tbsp chicken stock

4 tbsp dry cider

1 tbsp chopped fresh parsley

STUFFING

25 g/1 oz butter

2 shallots, finely chopped

1 celery stick, finely chopped

1 cooking apple, peeled,
cored and diced

SAUCE

1 shallot, very finely chopped

300 ml/10 fl oz dry cider

125 ml/4 fl oz chicken stock

1 tsp cider vinegar

NUTRITIONAL INFORMATION

Calories	.220
Protein	.30g
Carbohydrate	.13g
Sugars	.13g
Fat	.4g
Saturates	.2g

---

variation

Use 1.3 kg/3 lb whole chicken instead. Fill the neck with stuffing and roast for 1½ hours. Roll remaining stuffing into balls and bake for 15 minutes.

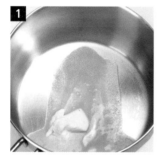

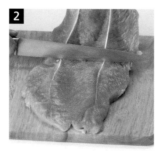

cook's tip

If you want to prepare part of this dish in advance, make the stuffing the day before and keep in the refrigerator until required.

1 Preheat the oven to 190°C/375°F/Gas Mark 5. To make the stuffing, melt the butter in a saucepan. Add the shallots and cook for 5 minutes. Add the celery and apple and cook for 5 minutes. Add the remaining stuffing ingredients, cover and simmer for 5 minutes, or until all the liquid has been absorbed. Transfer to a bowl and cool.

2 Place the roast on a chopping board and slice almost completely through, from the thin side towards the thicker side. Open out, place between 2 sheets of clingfilm and flatten with a meat mallet or rolling pin to an even thickness. Season with salt. Spoon on the cooled stuffing, roll the roast around it and tie with kitchen string.

Heat the oil in a roasting tin over a medium heat, add the roast and brown. Transfer to the oven and roast for 1 hour 10 minutes, or until cooked through and the juices run clear when the meat is pierced with a skewer.

3 Remove the roast from the tin and cover with foil. To make the sauce, pour

off any fat from the tin and set over a medium heat. Add the shallot and half the cider and cook for 1–2 minutes, scraping any sediment from the base of the tin. Add the remaining cider, stock and vinegar and cook for 10 minutes, or until reduced and thickened. Remove and discard the string from the turkey and cut into slices. Serve with the sauce.

vegetable & tofu stir-fry

serves 4   **prep: 10 mins,**   **cook: 12 mins**
plus 2 hrs marinating

Tofu, also known as bean curd, is a low-fat source of high-quality protein for vegetarians. Although it is naturally bland, it absorbs the flavours of other ingredients, especially if it is marinated. Store tofu in the refrigerator, covered with cold water, for up to 3 days, changing the water daily. Drain and pat dry before use.

INGREDIENTS

225 g/8 oz firm tofu (drained weight),
cut into bite-sized pieces
1 tbsp groundnut or sunflower oil
2 spring onions, chopped
1 garlic clove, finely chopped
115 g/4 oz baby corn cobs, halved
115 g/4 oz mangetout
115 g/4 oz shiitake mushrooms,
thinly sliced
2 tbsp finely chopped fresh
coriander leaves

MARINADE
2 tbsp dark soy sauce
1 tbsp Chinese rice wine
2 tsp brown sugar
½ tsp Chinese five-spice powder
1 fresh red chilli, deseeded and
finely chopped
2 spring onions, finely chopped
1 tbsp grated fresh root ginger

NUTRITIONAL INFORMATION

Calories	135
Protein	. . . . .11g
Carbohydrate	. . . . .7g
Sugars	. . . . .5g
Fat	. . . . .7g
Saturates	. . . . .3g

variation

Substitute baby carrots, celery and courgettes, cut into batons, for the baby corn cobs and mangetout.

cook's tip

Always drain firm tofu, because it is packaged in water. Use a small, sharp knife for cutting the tofu – a blunt knife will squash it.

1 Place all the marinade ingredients in a large, shallow, non-metallic dish and stir to mix. Add the bite-sized chunks of tofu and turn them over carefully to coat thoroughly in the marinade. Cover the dish with clingfilm and leave the tofu in the refrigerator to marinate for 2 hours, turning the chunks over once or twice.

2 Drain the tofu and reserve the marinade. Heat the groundnut oil in a preheated wok or large frying pan. Add the tofu and stir-fry over a medium–high heat for 2–3 minutes, or until golden. Using a slotted spoon, remove the tofu from the wok and set aside. Add the spring onions and garlic and stir-fry for 2 minutes, then add the corn cobs and stir-fry for 1 minute. Add the mangetout and mushrooms and stir-fry for a further 2 minutes.

3 Return the tofu to the wok and add the marinade. Cook gently for 1–2 minutes, or until heated through. Sprinkle with the chopped fresh coriander and serve immediately.

moroccan vegetable stew

serves 4 | **prep: 25 mins** | **cook: 45 mins**

This colourful selection of vegetables is simmered in a stock flavoured with lots of warming and aromatic spices.

INGREDIENTS

425 g/15 oz canned chickpeas

4 tomatoes, peeled and deseeded

700 ml/1¼ pints Vegetable Stock
(see page 11)

1 onion, peeled and sliced

2 carrots, peeled and sliced diagonally

1 tbsp chopped fresh coriander

salt

175 g/6 oz courgettes, sliced

1 small turnip, peeled and cubed

½ tsp ground turmeric

¼ tsp ground ginger

¼ tsp ground cinnamon

225 g/8 oz couscous

fresh coriander sprigs, to garnish

NUTRITIONAL INFORMATION

Calories 299

Protein 13g

Carbohydrate 56g

Sugars 7g

Fat 4g

Saturates 0g

cook's tip

You can also cook the couscous by putting it into a large heatproof bowl and pouring over enough boiling water to cover. Leave to stand for 5–8 minutes, then fluff up with a fork and serve.

1 Drain the chickpeas, rinse under cold running water and set aside. Roughly chop the tomatoes and reserve half. Place the remainder in a blender or food processor and process until a smooth purée forms. Transfer to a large saucepan and add 400 ml/14 fl oz of the vegetable stock. Bring to the boil, then reduce the heat and

add the onion, carrots, chopped fresh coriander and salt to taste. Simmer, stirring occasionally, for 10 minutes.

2 Stir in the courgettes, turnip, turmeric, ginger and cinnamon. Partially cover and simmer for a further 30 minutes. Stir in the reserved chickpeas and simmer for a few more minutes.

3 Meanwhile, bring the remaining vegetable stock to the boil in a heavy-based saucepan. Add a pinch of salt, then sprinkle in the couscous, stirring constantly. Remove the saucepan from the heat, cover with a tight-fitting lid and leave to stand for 5 minutes. Fluff up the couscous with a fork and transfer to 4 serving plates.

Top with the vegetables and their stock, garnish with a few sprigs of fresh coriander and serve immediately.

stuffed cabbage rolls

⏲ **cook: 1 hr 10 mins**   ⏱ **prep: 30 mins**   **serves 4**

*Bathed in a sweet tomato sauce, these cabbage rolls are stuffed
with a nutty filling of pearl barley and courgettes.*

NUTRITIONAL INFORMATION	
Calories	.224
Protein	.6g
Carbohydrate	.43g
Sugars	.19g
Fat	.5g
Saturates	.1g

INGREDIENTS

8 large or 12 medium green
cabbage leaves

1 litre/1¾ pints water

100 g/3½ oz pearl barley

2 tbsp chopped fresh parsley

2 garlic cloves, roughly chopped

800 g/1 lb 12 oz canned chopped tomatoes

4 tbsp red wine vinegar

1 tbsp sunflower or corn oil, plus

extra for brushing

2 courgettes, diced

3 spring onions, sliced

salt and pepper

2 tbsp brown sugar

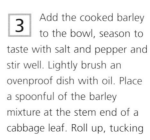

cook's tip

Substitute the pearl barley
with long-grain rice. Cook the
rice with half the parsley in
a large saucepan of boiling
water for 18–20 minutes in
Step 1. Drain and proceed as
in main recipe.

1 Preheat the oven to
190°C/375°F/Gas Mark
5. Cut out the stems from the
cabbage leaves, then blanch
the leaves in boiling water for
1 minute. Drain and spread
out to dry. Bring the water to
the boil in a saucepan. Add
the barley and half the parsley.
Reduce the heat, cover and
simmer for 45 minutes, or until
the liquid has been absorbed.

2 Meanwhile, put the
garlic, 400 g/14 oz of
the tomatoes and the vinegar
in a blender or food processor
and process until smooth.
Transfer to a bowl and set
aside. Heat the oil in a large
frying pan. Add the courgettes
and the remaining parsley and
cook over a medium heat for
3 minutes. Add the spring
onions and cook briefly, then

add the tomato mixture and
cook for 10 minutes, or until
thickened. Transfer to a bowl.

3 Add the cooked barley
to the bowl, season to
taste with salt and pepper and
stir well. Lightly brush an
ovenproof dish with oil. Place
a spoonful of the barley
mixture at the stem end of a
cabbage leaf. Roll up, tucking

in the sides, and place, seam-
side down, in the dish. Stuff
and roll the remaining cabbage
leaves in the same way, placing
them in the dish in a single
layer. Sprinkle the brown sugar
over the rolls and pour the
remaining tomatoes, with their
can juice, on top. Cover with
foil and bake in the oven for
30 minutes, or until tender.
Serve straight from the dish.

fish & shellfish

The perfect choice for healthy eating, all fish and shellfish – even so-called oily fish –

are naturally low in fat. Nutritionists recommend that we should eat fish two or three times a

week, and the recipes featured in this chapter will make that both easy and pleasurable to do.

Fish and shellfish are among the most versatile of ingredients and go well with a wide range

of vegetables, herbs and spices, and with cheese, pasta and rice. The huge choice of fish

available today ensures that there is a dish to suit all tastes and budgets.

Recipes range from familiar favourites, such as Smoked Haddock Pie (see page 124)

and Mussels in White Wine (see page 138) to more unusual dishes, such as Cajun-spiced Fish

(see page 132) and Sea Trout in a Salt Crust (see page 133). There are fabulous fish stews, such

as Louisiana Gumbo (see page 128), hot and spicy dishes, such as Indian Chilli Fish

(see page 127), easy midweek suppers, such as Cod with Cheese & Tomatoes (see page 120),

and flamboyant combinations for entertaining, such as Bouillabaisse (see page 136).

In many of the recipes, there is no reason why you shouldn't substitute your own

favourite fish for the one suggested. If sole seems too extravagant, use plaice or brill. If you can't

find swordfish steaks, try the same recipe with the humble cod. If you are lucky enough to find

affordable fresh langoustines, use them in one of the prawn recipes. The happy fact is that,

whatever fish you choose, you will be cooking a delicious and low-fat dish.

cod provençal

serves 4   **prep: 10 mins**    **cook: 15 mins**

Easy to prepare and easy to eat – that is the keynote to this tasty fish dish. As it is also packed with protein and vitamins and contains hardly any saturated fat, you could not make a better choice for a quick and healthy midweek supper.

INGREDIENTS

4 cod steaks, about 140 g/5 oz each

150 ml/5 fl oz Fish Stock

(see page 11)

1 bay leaf

6 black peppercorns

strip of thinly pared lemon rind

2 thin slices of onion

SAUCE

400 g/14 oz canned chopped tomatoes

1 garlic clove, very finely chopped

1 tbsp sun-dried tomato purée

1 tbsp capers, drained and rinsed

16 black olives, stoned

salt and pepper

GARNISH

fresh flat-leaved parsley sprigs

lemon wedges

NUTRITIONAL INFORMATION

Calories 168

Protein 23g

Carbohydrate 4g

Sugars 3g

Fat 7g

Saturates 1g

variation

Add a dash of Pernod to the tomato sauce in Step 3 to give the dish a little extra flavour.

cook's tip

If you don't have any freshly made fish stock, you can use a mixture of equal parts dry white wine and water, which works just as well.

1 First, make the sauce. Put the chopped tomatoes, garlic, tomato purée, capers, olives and salt and pepper to taste in a large, heavy-based saucepan over a low heat. Heat gently, stirring occasionally.

2 Meanwhile, place the fish in a shallow, flameproof casserole in a single layer. Pour in the fish stock and add the bay leaf, peppercorns, lemon rind and onion slices. Bring to the boil, then reduce the heat to very low, cover and simmer gently for 10 minutes, or until the fish is opaque and flakes easily when tested with the point of a knife. Using a fish slice, transfer the cod to a serving plate and keep warm.

3 Sieve the fish stock into the sauce and stir over a medium heat until slightly reduced. Pour the sauce over the fish, then garnish with a few sprigs of fresh parsley and lemon wedges. Serve.

serves 4 **prep: 20 mins** **cook: 8–10 mins**

Although they can be awkward and time-consuming to deal with, fresh sardines are a real treat. They are best cooked very simply – even just gutted and grilled or barbecued. Here they are flavoured with garlic and lemon rind and served with bruschetta. They would go well with a tomato and onion salad.

INGREDIENTS

1 tbsp olive oil

4 garlic cloves

650 g/1 lb 7 oz fresh sardines, gutted and scaled (see Cook's Tip)

grated rind of 2 lemons

2 tbsp chopped fresh flat-leaved parsley

salt and pepper

tomato and onion salad, to serve

BRUSCHETTA

4 thick slices of ciabatta or other rustic bread

2 garlic cloves, halved

2 large tomatoes, halved

NUTRITIONAL INFORMATION

Calories 405

Protein 38g

Carbohydrate 23g

Sugars 4g

Fat 19g

Saturates 5g

variation

A variety of toppings can be used for the bruschetta. Try grilled pepper with fresh basil. Replace the ciabatta with French bread slices.

cook's tip

Gutting sardines is easy. Slit open the belly and remove the insides. Rinse and dry. To scale, hold the fish by its tail under running water and run your hand along the body from tail to head.

1 Preheat the grill to medium. Heat the olive oil in a large, heavy-based frying pan. Add the garlic and cook over a low heat until softened. Meanwhile, for the bruschetta, put the bread under the preheated hot grill and toast lightly on both sides. Transfer to a heatproof plate and keep warm in a low oven until required.

2 Add the sardines to the frying pan and cook for 5 minutes, turning once. Sprinkle with the grated lemon rind and chopped fresh parsley and season to taste with salt and pepper.

3 To finish the bruschetta, rub 1 side of each slice of toast with the cut side of a garlic clove, then with the cut side of a tomato. Divide the bruschetta and sardines between 4 serving plates and serve immediately with a tomato and onion salad.

cod with cheese & tomatoes

serves 4

prep: 10 mins, plus 30 mins marinating

cook: 25 mins

Fish and cheese have a natural affinity, but recipes usually suggest adding creamy sauces with the result that the fat content begins to soar. Here, fish is oven-baked, topped with haloumi and grilled.

INGREDIENTS

4 cod or other firm white fish fillets,
about 175 g/6 oz each

grated rind and juice of 1 orange

8 canned anchovy fillets,
drained and patted dry

175 g/6 oz haloumi cheese

4 beef tomato slices

fresh parsley sprigs, to garnish

NUTRITIONAL INFORMATION

Calories	159
Protein	19g
Carbohydrate	6g
Sugars	6g
Fat	7g
Saturates	4g

cook's tip

Citrus juices will begin to 'cure' fish after 1 hour, so make sure that you don't leave the fish to marinate for too long.

1 Place the fish in a large, shallow, non-metallic flameproof dish. Sprinkle with the orange rind and pour the juice over it. Cover with clingfilm and leave to marinate in the refrigerator for 30 minutes.

2 Preheat the oven to 180°C/350°F/Gas Mark 4. Remove the clingfilm

and re-cover the dish with foil. Bake in the preheated oven for 15–20 minutes, or until the flesh flakes easily.

3 Preheat the grill to medium. Drain the anchovy fillets on kitchen paper and arrange 2 fillets on each piece of cod. Place under a preheated grill for 1 minute. Cut the haloumi cheese into

4 slices and place 1 slice on top of each cod fillet. Top with the tomato slices and return to the grill for a further 1–2 minutes, or until the cheese has charred slightly and the tomato is beginning to soften. Transfer to a serving plate, garnish with a few sprigs of fresh parsley and serve immediately.

fish balls in easy tomato sauce

⏱ **cook: 15 mins**   🕐 **prep: 15 mins**   **serves 4**

White fish can often taste rather bland so, in this dish, fresh herbs and spices and a chunky tomato sauce give a burst of extra flavour to wake up the taste buds.

NUTRITIONAL INFORMATION

Calories 134

Protein 22g

Carbohydrate 9g

Sugars 3g

Fat 1g

Saturates 0g

INGREDIENTS

few lengths of fresh chives

few sprigs of fresh dill

450 g/1 lb white fish fillets, skinned

salt and pepper

4 tbsp fresh wholemeal breadcrumbs

SAUCE

55 g/2 oz button mushrooms, sliced

400 g/14 oz canned chopped tomatoes

½ tsp ground cinnamon

½ tsp ground cumin

1 tbsp lemon juice

cook's tip

Use whiting, haddock, ling or even smoked haddock or smoked cod to make the fish balls. If you are making them for children, you can omit the spices.

1 Using a pair of kitchen scissors, snip the chives into short lengths, then snip the dill into small pieces. Reserve some herbs for the garnish. Check that there are no small bones remaining in the fish, removing any you find using tweezers. Season to taste with salt and pepper. Cut the fish into chunks and place in a food processor with the breadcrumbs, chives and dill. Process until the fish is finely chopped and the ingredients are mixed. Transfer to a bowl.

2 Take small pieces of the mixture and form into 16 walnut-sized balls.

3 To make the sauce, chop the mushrooms into thin slices, then add to a saucepan with the tomatoes and their can juice. Stir in the ground cinnamon and cumin. Bring to the boil, then reduce the heat and simmer. Add the fish balls and lemon juice, cover and cook over a very low heat for 10 minutes. Transfer to a large serving dish, garnish with the reserved herbs and serve.

sweet & sour fish

serves 4   **prep: 10 mins**   **cook: 35 mins**

*East meets West with this delicious fish bake. The combination
of the dark soy sauce, pineapple and peppers gives the fish a
wonderful flavour, and is a real treat on any occasion.*

INGREDIENTS

1 red pepper	225 g/8 oz canned pineapple
1 green pepper	cubes in syrup
3 tbsp dark soy sauce	2 tomatoes, peeled and chopped
4 tbsp white wine vinegar	175 g/6 oz button mushrooms,
1 tbsp tomato purée	thinly sliced
225 ml/8 fl oz Fish Stock	salt and pepper
(see page 11) or water	650 g/1 lb 7 oz white
2 tsp cornflour	fish fillets, skinned

(see page 11)

NUTRITIONAL INFORMATION

Calories	.192
Protein	.30g
Carbohydrate	.16g
Sugars	.14g
Fat	.2g
Saturates	.0g

variation

You can use any firm-fleshed white
fish fillets in this dish. Try haddock,
cod, monkfish or whiting.

cook's tip

To skin a fish fillet, secure it
on a board with salt. Insert a
sharp, flexible knife at one
end and hold firmly. Move
the knife along the length of
the fillet in a cutting motion
against the skin.

1 Preheat the oven
to 180°C/350°/Gas
Mark 4. Prepare the peppers.
Using a sharp knife, halve each
pepper, remove the core,
deseed and cut into batons.
Put the soy sauce, vinegar and
tomato purée in a saucepan.
Put 4 tablespoons of the fish
stock in a small bowl and add
the remainder to the
saucepan. Stir the cornflour

into the reserved fish stock to
make a smooth paste. Bring
the mixture in the saucepan to
the boil, stir in the cornflour
paste and cook over a low
heat, stirring, until thickened.
Simmer for 5 minutes.

2 Add the reserved
peppers, pineapple
cubes and syrup, tomatoes and
mushrooms to the saucepan

and cook, stirring occasionally,
for 5 minutes. Season to taste
with salt and pepper

3 Arrange the fish fillets
in the base of a
shallow ovenproof dish. Spoon
the sauce mixture on top and
cover with foil. Bake in the
oven for 20 minutes, or until
the fish flakes easily. Serve.

smoked haddock pie

serves 4　　　　**prep: 15 mins**　　　　**cook: 50 mins**

Real comfort food, fish pie is a family favourite and there is no reason to go without. Using skimmed milk and reduced-fat cheese won't affect the flavour adversely, but will ensure a healthier meal.

INGREDIENTS

750 g/1 lb 10 oz floury potatoes, cut into chunks

salt and pepper

450 g/1 lb smoked haddock fillets

600 ml/1 pint skimmed milk

4 juniper berries

4 black peppercorns

1 bay leaf

2 tbsp plain flour

325 g/11½ oz canned sweetcorn, drained

25 g/1 oz butter

55 g/2 oz reduced-fat Cheddar cheese, grated

fresh flat-leaved parsley sprigs, to garnish

NUTRITIONAL INFORMATION

Calories	.478
Protein	.38g
Carbohydrate	.69g
Sugars	.17g
Fat	.7g
Saturates	.4g

variation

For a slightly different fish pie, try substituting smoked cod, whiting or coley for the smoked haddock.

cook's tip

For the healthiest choice, look for naturally pale smoked haddock, rather than the bright yellow dyed fish, and canned sweetcorn with no added salt or sugar.

1 Preheat the oven to 200°C/400°F/Gas Mark 6. Cook the potatoes in a large saucepan of lightly salted boiling water for 20 minutes, or until tender. Meanwhile, place the fish in a large frying pan, pour in the milk and add the juniper berries, peppercorns and bay leaf. Cover and simmer over a low heat for 10 minutes, or until the flesh flakes easily. Transfer the fish to a chopping board. Sieve the milk and set aside. When the fish is cool enough to handle, remove and discard the skin and any small remaining bones. Flake the flesh and place in a bowl.

2 Place the flour in a saucepan and gradually whisk in 400 ml/14 fl oz of the reserved milk, setting the rest aside. Bring to the boil over a low heat, stirring, then simmer for 1 minute. Season to taste with salt and pepper. Add the sauce to the fish with the sweetcorn, then spoon into an ovenproof dish.

3 When the potatoes are tender, drain well, then mash with the butter and remaining milk. Spoon the mash over the fish, spreading it out to cover. Sprinkle the cheese on top and bake in the oven for 25–30 minutes, or until golden. Serve immediately, garnished with parsley sprigs.

kedgeree

serves 4   **prep: 15 mins**   **cook: 40 mins**

Derived from an Indian dish of rice, onions, lentils and eggs, kedgeree dates from the days of the British Raj. Fish was added and kedgeree became a staple for leisurely colonial breakfasts.

INGREDIENTS

225-g/8-oz haddock fillet
225-g/8-oz smoked haddock fillet
1 tbsp sunflower or corn oil
1 onion, chopped
½ tsp ground turmeric
½ tsp ground cumin
½ tsp chilli powder
¼ tsp ground ginger
225 g/8 oz long-grain rice
salt and pepper

GARNISH
1 hard-boiled egg
2 tbsp chopped fresh parsley

NUTRITIONAL INFORMATION

Calories 340

Protein 27g

Carbohydrate 47g

Sugars 1g

Fat 5g

Saturates 1g

variation

Traditionally, 150 ml/5 fl oz single or soured cream is folded in with the fish. An alternative would be to use the same quantity of low-fat natural yogurt.

1 Place the haddock fillets in a large, heavy-based frying pan. Pour in enough water to cover and poach gently over a low heat for 10–15 minutes, or until the flesh flakes easily. Remove the fish with a fish slice and leave to cool. Sieve the cooking liquid into a measuring jug and make up to 600 ml/1 pint, if necessary.

2 Heat the oil in a flameproof casserole. Add the onion and cook over a low heat for 3 minutes, or until soft. Stir in the spices, then the rice, and cook, stirring, until well coated. Stir in the reserved cooking liquid. Bring to the boil, cover and cook over a low heat for 20 minutes, or until all the liquid has been absorbed and the rice is tender.

3 Meanwhile, skin the fish and remove any remaining bones. Flake the flesh. Fold the fish into the rice, season to taste with salt and pepper and transfer to a large, warmed serving dish. Shell the hard-boiled egg and cut into quarters, then use to garnish the kedgeree. Sprinkle with chopped fresh parsley and serve immediately.

indian chilli fish

cook: 10 mins **prep: 10 mins, plus 30 mins marinating** **serves 4**

The lime juice in this Indian-style recipe helps protect the delicate flesh of the fish from the fierce heat of the grill during cooking. However, keep an eye open and lower the heat if it seems too dry.

NUTRITIONAL INFORMATION

Calories 144

Protein 21g

Carbohydrate 3g

Sugars 3g

Fat 5g

Saturates 1g

INGREDIENTS

1-cm/½-inch piece fresh root ginger

4 plaice fillets, about 115 g/4 oz each

1 tbsp groundnut or sunflower oil

1 tbsp chopped fresh coriander

2 tbsp lime juice

300 ml/10 fl oz water

2 tbsp tomato purée

1 tbsp chilli sauce

1 tbsp white wine vinegar

1 tsp muscovado sugar

fresh coriander sprigs, to garnish

lime wedges, to serve

variation

This sauce is delicious with prawns. Add 450 g/1 lb cooked, peeled prawns to the sauce to heat through during the last 2–3 minutes of cooking.

1 Grate the ginger and set aside. Place the fish in a shallow, non-metallic dish. Pour in the groundnut oil, chopped coriander and lime juice and turn the fish to coat well. Cover with clingfilm and leave to marinate in the refrigerator for 30 minutes.

2 Preheat the grill to medium. Put the water, tomato purée, chilli sauce, vinegar, grated ginger and sugar in a small saucepan. Bring to the boil over a low heat, stirring. Simmer, stirring occasionally, for 5–8 minutes, or until thickened.

3 Meanwhile, remove the fish from the marinade and cook under the grill for 5–8 minutes, or until the flesh is opaque and flakes easily. Transfer to 4 serving plates and spoon over the sauce. Garnish with coriander sprigs and serve with lime wedges.

louisiana gumbo

Transport yourself and your guests to Louisiana with this fabulous fish stew. There is an almost infinite number of recipes for this traditional dish, but they are all thickened with okra, a small green seed pod with a sticky juice that gives the stew a silky finish.

NUTRITIONAL INFORMATION

Calories	240
Protein	. . . . .35g
Carbohydrate	. . . . .12g
Sugars	. . . . .6g
Fat	. . . . .6g
Saturates	. . . . .1g

INGREDIENTS

2 tbsp sunflower or corn oil

175 g/6 oz okra, trimmed and cut into

2.5-cm/1-inch pieces

2 onions, very finely chopped

4 celery sticks, very finely chopped

1 garlic clove, finely chopped

2 tbsp plain flour

½ tsp sugar

1 tsp ground cumin

salt and pepper

700 ml/1¼ pints Fish Stock

(see page 11)

1 red pepper, deseeded and chopped

1 green pepper, deseeded and chopped

2 large tomatoes

350 g/12 oz large raw prawns

4 tbsp chopped fresh parsley

1 tbsp chopped fresh coriander

dash of Tabasco sauce

350-g/12-oz cod or haddock

fillet, skinned and cut into

2.5-cm/1-inch cubes

350-g/12-oz monkfish fillet, cut

into 2.5-cm/1-inch cubes

variation

For a filé gumbo, add 1 teaspoon filé powder with the flour in Step 1 to thicken and flavour the stew. (Filé powder is made from sassafras leaves.)

cook's tip

To peel and devein prawns, remove the head and tail, then peel away the shell. Using a sharp knife, cut along the back of the prawn to remove the black intestinal thread that runs down the centre. Wash well.

1 Heat half the oil in a large, flameproof casserole. Add the okra and cook over a low heat, stirring frequently, for 5 minutes, or until browned. Remove from the casserole and set aside. Add the remaining oil and the onion and celery and cook, stirring occasionally, for 5 minutes, or until softened. Add the garlic and cook for

1 minute. Stir in the flour, sugar and cumin and season to taste with salt and pepper. Cook, stirring, for 2 minutes, then gradually stir in the fish stock and bring to the boil, stirring constantly.

2 Return the reserved okra to the casserole and add the peppers and tomatoes. Partially cover,

reduce the heat to very low and simmer gently, stirring occasionally, for 10 minutes. Peel and devein the prawns (see Cook's Tip) and set aside.

3 Add the parsley and coriander and Tabasco sauce to taste, then gently stir in the fish and peeled prawns. Cover and simmer gently for 5 minutes, or until the fish is

cooked through and the prawns have changed colour. Transfer to a large, warmed serving dish and serve.

halibut parcels

serves 4 **prep: 20 mins** **cook: 10–15 mins**

Cooking in a parcel is an excellent low-fat technique that works especially well with fish, as it protects the delicate flesh. It is also a very attractive way to present a main meal.

INGREDIENTS

4 baby leeks, cut into thin strips

4 baby courgettes, cut into thin batons

4 baby carrots, cut into thin batons

1 fennel bulb, halved and

cut into thin strips

115 g/4 oz chanterelle mushrooms,

thinly sliced

2 tbsp finely chopped fresh chervil

salt and pepper

4 halibut steaks, about 175 g/6 oz each

4 tsp extra virgin olive oil

4 tbsp white wine

NUTRITIONAL INFORMATION	
Calories	234
Protein	33g
Carbohydrate	6g
Sugars	3g
Fat	8g
Saturates	1g

variation

Substitute 2 canned artichoke hearts, drained, for the fennel strips, and replace the halibut steaks with salmon steaks.

1 Preheat the oven to 190°C/375°F/Gas Mark 5. Cut out 4 x 30-cm/ 12-inch squares of baking paper and spread out on a work surface.

2 Divide the leeks, courgettes, carrots, fennel and mushrooms equally among the paper squares. Sprinkle with half the chervil and season to taste with salt and pepper. Top each bed of vegetables with a halibut steak and sprinkle with the remaining herbs. Fold up the edges of the paper, but do not seal. Drizzle 1 teaspoon of olive oil and 1 tablespoon of wine over each fish steak, then fold over the edges of the paper to seal and make a loosely wrapped parcel.

3 Place the parcels on a baking sheet and bake in the preheated oven for 10–15 minutes, or until the parcels are puffed up. Transfer the parcels to 4 large, warmed serving plates and serve.

baked lemon sole

⏲ **cook: 15 mins**   ◔ **prep: 5 mins**   **serves 4**

A simple mixture of herbs, lemon juice and garlic is delicious, but will not overwhelm the delicate flavour of the fish. Serve with freshly cooked rice and vegetables for a filling supper.

NUTRITIONAL INFORMATION

Calories 193

Protein 30g

Carbohydrate 0g

Sugars 0g

Fat 8g

Saturates 1g

INGREDIENTS

2 garlic cloves

4 lemon sole fillets,
about 175 g/6 oz each

1 shallot, finely chopped

2 fresh lemon thyme sprigs, plus
extra to garnish

2 fresh lemon balm sprigs, plus
extra to garnish

salt and pepper

grated rind and juice of 1 lemon

2 tbsp extra virgin olive oil

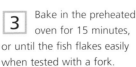

cook's tip

Lemon sole is not related to Dover sole and is less expensive, but still has a fine flavour and delicate flesh. It is available from most large supermarkets.

1 Preheat the oven to 180°C/350°F/Gas Mark 4. Using a sharp knife, thinly slice the garlic and set aside.

2 Arrange the sole fillets in a single layer in the base of a large ovenproof dish and sprinkle with the shallot. Place the reserved garlic slices and fresh herb sprigs on top of the fillets and season to taste with salt and pepper. Mix the lemon juice and olive oil together in a small jug and pour it over the fish.

3 Bake in the preheated oven for 15 minutes, or until the fish flakes easily when tested with a fork.

Sprinkle with lemon rind, garnish with the extra fresh herbs and serve immediately.

cajun-spiced fish

serves 4   **prep: 5 mins**   **cook: 10 mins**

Descended from immigrant French cuisine, Cajun cooking is marked with a practical approach that makes the most of the locally available ingredients in the countryside around New Orleans.

INGREDIENTS

1 tbsp lime juice

2 tbsp low-fat natural yogurt

4 swordfish steaks, about 175 g/6 oz each

sunflower or corn oil, for brushing

lemon wedges, to serve

SPICE MIX

1 tsp paprika

1 tsp cayenne pepper

1 tsp ground cumin

1 tsp mustard powder

1 tsp dried oregano

NUTRITIONAL INFORMATION

Calories 215

Protein 33g

Carbohydrate 2g

Sugars 2g

Fat 8g

Saturates 2g

cook's tip

Brush the fish steaks lightly with oil and cook under a preheated hot grill or on a lit barbecue instead. Brush again with oil when you turn them.

1 First make the spice mix by blending all the ingredients in a bowl. Mix the lime juice and yogurt in a separate bowl.

2 Pat the fish steaks dry with kitchen paper, then brush both sides with the yogurt mixture. Use your hands to coat both sides of the fish with the spice mix, rubbing it well into the flesh.

3 Brush a griddle pan with a little sunflower oil. Add the fish steaks and cook for 5 minutes over a medium heat, then turn over and cook for a further 4 minutes, or until the flesh flakes easily when tested with a fork. Serve straight from the pan with lemon wedges.

sea trout in a salt crust

⏲ **cook: 25 mins**   🕐 **prep: 20 mins, plus 10 mins standing**   **serves 4**

This is an unusual, but very effective, way to cook fish, sealing in all the delicate flavour of the sea trout. When you are ready to serve, simply break the crust and lift out the perfectly baked fish.

NUTRITIONAL INFORMATION

Calories	.282
Protein	.49g
Carbohydrate	.0g
Sugars	.2g
Fat	.9g
Saturates	.2g

INGREDIENTS

about 2 kg/4 lb 8 oz coarse

sea salt

1 tsp dried thyme

1 tsp dried rosemary

1 tsp dried dill

3 garlic cloves, very finely chopped

1 large egg white

4 whole sea trout,

about 300 g/10½ oz each

salt and pepper

2 fresh thyme sprigs

2 fresh rosemary sprigs

2 fresh dill sprigs

cook's tip

Choose firm fish with bright eyes and bright pink gills, which indicate freshness. Buy the fish on the day you want to cook it. Fresh fish should be stored in the refrigerator and used within 12 hours.

1 Preheat the oven to 240°C/475°F/Gas Mark 9. Mix the sea salt, dried herbs, garlic and egg white until all the salt crystals are moistened.

2 Using a sharp knife, slit the fish open along the belly and remove the innards. Rinse the fish inside and out under cold running water and

pat dry with kitchen paper. Season the cavity with salt and pepper to taste and place the fresh herbs inside. Line a large ovenproof dish with a double layer of foil, leaving an overhang, and make a thick layer of the salt mixture on the base. Place the fish on top and cover with remaining salt. Bring up the edges of the foil to enclose the salt.

3 Bake in the preheated oven for 25 minutes. Turn off the heat, but do not remove the dish for a further 10 minutes. To serve, carefully lift out the foil package, open up and break away all the salt crust, gently brushing off residual traces. Lift off the individual fish, transfer to 4 large serving plates and serve immediately.

caribbean snapper

serves 4 **prep: 15 mins, plus 30 mins marinating** ⏱ **cook: 20 mins** ⏱

Snapper is actually a large family of fish that range in colour from pink, through red, to orange. It is much prized in the Caribbean for its delicate flavour. Serve with corn bread for a complete meal.

INGREDIENTS

2 tbsp dark rum

50 ml/2 fl oz white wine

1 tbsp finely chopped fresh root ginger

1 garlic clove, finely chopped

salt and pepper

500 g/1 lb 2 oz red snapper fillets

1 onion

1 tbsp corn or sunflower oil

2 tbsp plain flour

2 tsp tomato purée

1 red pepper, deseeded and roughly chopped

500 ml/18 fl oz Fish Stock (see page 11)

2 large tomatoes, skinned, deseeded and roughly chopped

1 mango, peeled, stoned and roughly chopped

variation

Add 140 g/5 oz canned sweetcorn, drained, and substitute 280 g/10 oz peeled diced pumpkin for the mango.

cook's tip

Don't skin the fish fillets before cooking as the pieces may fall apart. If red snapper is unavailable then use red mullet instead.

1 Mix the rum, wine, ginger and garlic in a shallow, non-metallic dish and season to taste with pepper. Cut the fish fillets into 4-cm/1½-inch pieces and add to the marinade. Using a spoon, carefully coat the fish with the marinade. Cover with clingfilm and leave in the refrigerator to marinate for 30 minutes.

2 Remove the fish using a slotted spoon and set aside. Reserve the marinade. Using a sharp knife, cut the onion into wedges. Heat the oil in a large saucepan, add the onion wedges and cook over a medium heat, stirring occasionally, for 5 minutes, or until just beginning to brown. Stir in the flour and add the tomato purée and red pepper.

Gradually stir in the fish stock and the reserved marinade and bring to the boil, stirring constantly. Reduce the heat and simmer for 3 minutes.

3 Add the fish, tomatoes and mango to the saucepan and season to taste with salt. Cover and simmer for 8 minutes, or until the fish flakes easily, then serve.

bouillabaisse

serves 8

prep: 30 mins, plus 30 mins marinating

cook: 20 mins

This is probably the most famous fish stew in the world and just about every French village on the Mediterranean coastline has its own particular version. A good-quality fish stock is absolutely essential. Serve with plenty of French bread.

INGREDIENTS

1.25 kg/2 lb 12 oz sea bass, filleted, skinned and cut into bite-sized pieces

1.25 kg/2 lb 12 oz redfish, filleted, skinned and cut into bite-sized pieces

3 tbsp extra virgin olive oil

grated rind of 1 orange

1 garlic clove, finely chopped

pinch of saffron threads

2 tbsp pastis

450 g/1 lb live mussels

1 large cooked crab

1 small fennel bulb, finely chopped

2 celery sticks, finely chopped

1 onion, finely chopped

1.2 litres/2 pints Fish Stock (see page 11)

225 g/8 oz small new potatoes

225 g/8 oz tomatoes, peeled, deseeded and chopped

450 g/1 lb large raw prawns

salt and pepper

NUTRITIONAL INFORMATION

Calories 359

Protein 54g

Carbohydrate 7g

Sugars 2g

Fat 13g

Saturates 1g

variation

Replace the sea bass with whiting and substitute clams for the mussels. You could also add cooked, peeled prawns and garnish with whole cooked ones.

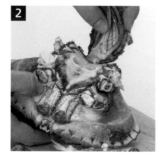

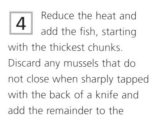

cook's tip

Redfish or Norwegian haddock is related to the scorpion fish. It is a traditional ingredient in bouillabaisse, but if you cannot find it, use red mullet instead.

1 Put the fish pieces in a large bowl and add 2 tablespoons of the olive oil, the orange rind, garlic, saffron and pastis. Turn the fish pieces to coat well, cover and leave in the refrigerator to marinate for 30 minutes.

2 Meanwhile, clean the mussels by scrubbing or scraping the shells and pulling out any beards that are attached to them. Remove the meat from the cooked crab and chop. Set aside.

3 Heat the remaining olive oil in a large flameproof casserole. Add the fennel, celery and onion and cook over a low heat, stirring occasionally, for 5 minutes, or until softened. Add the fish stock and bring to the boil. Add the new potatoes and tomatoes and cook over a medium heat for 7 minutes.

4 Reduce the heat and add the fish, starting with the thickest chunks. Discard any mussels that do not close when sharply tapped with the back of a knife and add the remainder to the stew. Add the prawns and pieces of crab and simmer until the fish is opaque, the mussels have opened again and the prawns have changed colour. Discard any mussels that remain closed. Season the bouillabaisse to taste with salt and pepper and serve immediately.

mussels in white wine

serves 4   **prep: 10 mins** ⏱   **cook: 15 mins** ⏱

Also known as moules marinière, this quick and simple dish is the perfect way to serve seaside-fresh mussels. However, do not gather them yourself, as they may be toxic from pollution in the sea.

INGREDIENTS

4 shallots

3 garlic cloves

25 g/1 oz butter

300 ml/10 fl oz dry white wine

1 bouquet garni

salt and pepper

2 kg/4½ lb live mussels, scrubbed and debearded

2 tbsp chopped fresh parsley

NUTRITIONAL INFORMATION

Calories 236

Protein 27g

Carbohydrate 3g

Sugars 2g

Fat 8g

Saturates 4g

variation

For moules marinière Normandy-style, substitute a good-quality dry cider for the wine. Replace the bouquet garni with sprigs of thyme and a bay leaf.

1 Using a sharp knife, chop the shallots finely, then crush the garlic. Set aside. Discard any mussels with broken shells, or any that refuse to close when tapped with a knife.

2 Melt the butter in a large saucepan. Add the shallots and garlic and cook over a low heat, stirring frequently, for 5 minutes, or until softened. Pour in the wine, add the bouquet garni and season to taste with salt and pepper. Bring to the boil over a medium heat and add the mussels. Cover and cook, shaking the saucepan frequently, for 5 minutes, or until the mussels have opened. Discard any mussels that remain closed.

3 Remove and discard the bouquet garni. Using a slotted spoon, divide the mussels between 4 soup bowls. Tilt the saucepan and spoon a little of the cooking liquid over each plate. Sprinkle with the chopped fresh parsley and serve immediately.

spaghetti with saffron mussels

⏲ **cook: 25 mins**   ⏱ **prep: 20 mins**   **serves 4**

This is a pasta dish with attitude – its elegant colour and sophisticated flavour put it in a class of its own, yet it is quick and easy to make, as well as a healthy and filling supper dish.

NUTRITIONAL INFORMATION

Calories 479

Protein 23g

Carbohydrate 76g

Sugars 6g

Fat 6g

Saturates 1g

INGREDIENTS

¼ tsp saffron threads

175 ml/6 fl oz water

900 g/2 lb live mussels, scrubbed
and debearded

125 ml/4 fl oz white wine

1 tbsp sunflower or corn oil

1 small onion, finely chopped

2 tbsp plain flour

150 ml/5 fl oz Noilly Prat or other
extra dry vermouth

350 g/12 oz dried spaghetti

2 tbsp snipped fresh dill

salt and pepper

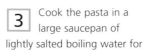

cook's tip

To prepare mussels, scrub under cold running water and scrape off all barnacles with a sharp knife. Tug off the beards. Discard any with broken shells and any that do not shut when tapped with a knife.

1 Gently crush the saffron threads and place in a bowl with the water. Leave to soak. Discard any mussels that do not close when sharply tapped with a knife, and put the remainder in a large saucepan. Add the wine and bring to the boil. Cover and cook over a high heat, shaking the saucepan occasionally, for 5 minutes, or until the mussels have opened. Remove the mussels with a slotted spoon, discarding any that remain closed. Sieve the cooking liquid through a muslin-lined sieve and reserve. When the mussels are cool enough to handle, remove from their shells.

2 Heat the oil in a heavy-based frying pan. Add the onion and cook over a low heat for 5 minutes, or until soft. Stir in the flour and cook, stirring, for 1 minute. Remove from the heat and add the vermouth and the soaking liquid, whisking constantly. Return to a low heat and cook for 2 minutes, until thickened.

3 Cook the pasta in a large saucepan of lightly salted boiling water for 8–10 minutes, until tender but firm to the bite. Meanwhile, place 4 tablespoons of the reserved cooking liquid in a pan and stir in the saffron mixture. Add the mussels and dill and season to taste with salt and pepper. Cook over a low heat until heated through. Drain the spaghetti, place in a large serving bowl and toss with the sauce. Serve immediately.

shellfish stew

serves 8   **prep: 20 mins** ⟳   **cook: 20 mins** ⟳

This is an ideal dish for an informal supper party, as it looks and tastes spectacular, yet is easy to make. Provide several empty dishes for collecting the shells, and bread for mopping up the juices.

INGREDIENTS

24 live mussels

24 clams

450 g/1 lb sea bream fillets

1.5 litres/2¾ pints Fish Stock

(see page 11)

225 ml/8 fl oz dry white wine

2 shallots, finely chopped

24 raw Mediterranean prawns,

peeled and deveined

700 g/1 lb 9 oz tomatoes, peeled,

deseeded and roughly chopped

3 tbsp snipped fresh chives

grated rind of 1 lemon

pinch of saffron threads

3 tbsp finely chopped fresh parsley

salt and pepper

variation

Sea bass would also work very well in this stew. If you cannot find the Mediterranean prawns, use ordinary prawns instead.

cook's tip

This dish is quite messy, so provide finger bowls filled with hot water and a slice of lemon so each guest can wash their fingers after eating.

1 Clean the mussels by scrubbing and scraping the shells and pulling out any beards that are attached to them. Discard any with broken shells, or that do not close when sharply tapped with a knife. Scrub the clams and discard any that do not close when tapped. Cut the sea bream into bite-sized pieces and set aside.

2 Pour the fish stock and wine into a large, heavy-based saucepan and bring to the boil. Add the mussels, clams and shallots, cover and cook over a medium heat for 4 minutes.

3 Sieve the shellfish, reserving the stock. Discard any mussels or clams that remain closed and set the

remainder aside. Rinse the saucepan and sieve the stock back into it through a muslin-lined sieve. Return to the boil and add the prawns and sea bream. Stir in the tomatoes, chives, lemon rind, saffron and parsley and season to taste. Cook over a low heat for 10 minutes, or until the fish flakes easily when tested with the point of a knife.

4 Remove the saucepan from the heat, add the mussels and clams, cover and leave to stand for 5 minutes. Divide the stew between 4 soup plates and serve.

rigatoni with squid

serves 4 **prep: 10 mins** **cook: 50 mins**

This delicious combination of pasta and squid is excellent for a light summer supper. If time is limited, use fresh pasta, as it takes less time to cook than dried. Farfalle and penne would also work well.

INGREDIENTS

1 red pepper	400 g/14 oz canned chopped tomatoes
1 yellow pepper	½–1 tsp chilli powder
1 tbsp sunflower or corn oil	250 g/9 oz dried rigatoni
350 g/12 oz prepared squid rings	2 tbsp chopped fresh basil
1 onion, chopped	salt and pepper
1 garlic clove, finely chopped	

NUTRITIONAL INFORMATION

Calories 349

Protein 23g

Carbohydrate 56g

Sugars 10g

Fat 5g

Saturates 0g

variation

Use fresh tomatoes instead of canned when they are in season. Peel, deseed and chop 750 g/1 lb 10 oz tomatoes and add them in Step 2.

cook's tip

The trick with squid is to cook it very rapidly. It is only tough and rubbery when it is over-cooked. If stir-frying, cook the squid for 2 minutes, until the rings are opaque.

1 Preheat the grill to medium. Place the peppers on a baking sheet and roast under the grill, turning frequently, for 15 minutes, or until charred and beginning to blacken. Remove with tongs, place in a polythene bag and seal the top. When the peppers are cool enough to handle, rub off the skins, deseed and chop the flesh.

2 Heat the oil in a heavy-based frying pan. Add the squid rings and stir-fry for 1–2 minutes, or until opaque. Remove the squid and set aside. Add the onion and garlic and cook for 5 minutes, or until soft. Add the tomatoes and peppers and chilli powder to taste, reduce the heat and simmer for 20–25 minutes, or until thickened.

3 Meanwhile, cook the pasta in a saucepan of lightly salted water for 8–10 minutes, or until tender but still firm to the bite. Just before serving, stir the squid rings and basil into the sauce and season to taste with salt and pepper. Heat through for 2–3 minutes. Drain the pasta, transfer to a serving dish and toss with the sauce. Serve.

prawn stir-fry

serves 4　　　**prep: 5 mins**　　　**cook: 8 mins**

This colourful dish takes hardly any time to prepare and cook, which makes it an ideal midweek supper. Serve with plain boiled rice or with freshly cooked noodles.

INGREDIENTS

8 spring onions

2 tbsp groundnut or sunflower oil

2 garlic cloves, very finely chopped

1 tbsp grated fresh root ginger

1 green pepper

1 red pepper

200 g/7 oz mangetout

450 g/1 lb raw tiger prawns, thawed if frozen, peeled and deveined

4 tbsp Chinese rice wine

NUTRITIONAL INFORMATION

Calories 203

Protein 28g

Carbohydrate 5g

Sugars 4g

Fat 8g

Saturates 1g

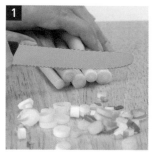

variation

Substitute thinly sliced broccoli florets for the mangetout for an equally colourful and tasty dish. Replace the Chinese rice wine with dry sherry.

1 Using a sharp knife, trim the spring onions and finely chop. Deseed and slice the peppers.

2 Heat the groundnut oil in a preheated wok or heavy-based frying pan. Add

the spring onions, garlic, ginger and peppers and stir-fry over a medium–high heat for 4 minutes.

3 Add the mangetout and prawns and stir-fry for 4 minutes, or until the prawns

have changed colour. Stir in the Chinese rice wine, then transfer to 4 large, warmed serving plates and serve.

mexican prawns

⏱ **cook: 20 mins**   ⏱ **prep: 5 mins**   **serves 4**

For a very special treat, you could use large or tiger prawns for this tasty dish. If the prawns are frozen, make sure that they are fully thawed out before you begin cooking.

NUTRITIONAL INFORMATION

Calories	.189
Protein	.27g
Carbohydrate	.9g
Sugars	.7g
Fat	.5g
Saturates	.1g

INGREDIENTS

1 fresh green chilli

1 tbsp sunflower or corn oil

1 large onion, finely chopped

3 garlic cloves, finely chopped

3 beef tomatoes, peeled, deseeded
and chopped

1 bay leaf

450 g/1 lb cooked, peeled prawns

1 tbsp lime juice

few sprigs of fresh coriander, plus
extra to garnish

salt and pepper

cook's tip

It is difficult to estimate how hot chillies are unless you know the variety, and even then, individual specimens may vary. Dark green chillies are usually hotter than pale green ones.

1 Using a sharp knife, cut the chilli in half and remove and discard the seeds, then chop finely and set aside.

2 Heat the sunflower oil in a heavy-based frying pan. Add the onion and garlic and cook over a low heat, stirring occasionally, for 5 minutes, or until softened.

3 Add the chopped tomatoes, chilli and bay leaf and simmer over a low heat, stirring occasionally, for 10 minutes, or until thickened.

4 Toss the prawns in the lime juice and stir into the sauce. Chop the coriander and stir into the sauce. Season to taste with salt and pepper.

Cook for a further 4 minutes, or until heated through. Transfer to 4 large serving bowls and garnish with fresh coriander sprigs. Serve.

hot & spicy prawns

serves 4   **prep: 20 mins** ⟲   **cook: 15 mins** ⟲

This is a fiery dish for lovers of chilli – so beware. You can reduce the number of chillies if you prefer a milder flavouring. Shrimp paste is available from Chinese food shops and large supermarkets.

INGREDIENTS

1 garlic clove

1-cm/½-inch cube shrimp paste

1-cm/½-inch piece fresh root ginger, thinly sliced

4 fresh red chillies, deseeded and finely chopped

1 tbsp groundnut or sunflower oil

4 spring onions, chopped

1 green pepper, deseeded and cut into thin batons

400 g/14 oz canned chopped tomatoes

1 tbsp brown sugar

50 ml/2 fl oz water (optional)

350 g/12 oz cooked, peeled prawns

3–4 spring onions, to garnish

NUTRITIONAL INFORMATION	
Calories	165
Protein	22g
Carbohydrate	10g
Sugars	10g
Fat	5g
Saturates	1g

variation

This sauce is also delicious with crab. Use 2 cooked crabs, weighing about 650 g/1 lb 7 oz. Remove the meat and add it in Step 3. Proceed as in recipe.

cook's tip

If you prepare the spring onions for the garnish before cooking, then place the shreds in a bowl of iced water to keep them fresh.

1 Peel and finely chop the garlic, then put it in a mortar with the shrimp paste, ginger and chillies. Using a pestle, grind to a paste. Heat the groundnut oil in a preheated wok or large, heavy-based frying pan and cook the spice paste over a medium heat, stirring constantly, for 1 minute. Do not let it brown.

2 Add the spring onions and green pepper and cook, stirring constantly, for 5 minutes, then stir in the tomatoes and sugar. Bring to the boil, stirring constantly. If the sauce is too thick, add the water. Reduce the heat and simmer for 5 minutes.

3 Stir in the prawns and cook for 4 minutes, or until heated through. Using a sharp knife, finely shred the spring onions for the garnish. Transfer the prawns to 4 large serving bowls, garnish with the shredded spring onions and serve immediately.

desserts & baking

For many people, a meal is not complete without a dessert, but they mistakenly believe that they must forego that pleasure when following a low-fat eating plan. For such people, this chapter will be a revelation. Treats for those with a sweet tooth include Hot Chocolate Cherries (see page 154), Banana Soufflés (see page 156) and Magic Cheesecake (see page 167). There are familiar delights, such as Stuffed Baked Apples (see page 153), and more unusual temptations, such as Indonesian Black Rice Pudding (see page 166). Fruit features in many guises, from simple Chargrilled Fruit (see page 150) to a pretty Fig & Watermelon Salad (see page 152). For summer time, there is a selection of refreshing iced desserts with a fraction of the fat found in traditional ice cream. Try Coffee Ice Cream (see page 162) to round off a dinner party, or Peach Sorbet (see page 164) after an alfresco lunch.

Home-baked cakes and biscuits are always popular, but they don't have to involve lashings of butter. If you still need convincing, just look at the wonderful Fat-free Marble Cake (see page 168) with its decorative chocolate and vanilla patterning. As its name suggests, it contains no fat at all. Other delicious low-fat confections include a marvellously moist and light Apricot Cake (see page 170) and Fruity Flapjacks (see page 173), both destined to become a firm family favourite.

chargrilled fruit

serves 4 **prep: 20 mins** **cook: 10 mins**

Fruit is the obvious choice for a low-fat dessert, but it can be rather unexciting. Liven it up with a flavoursome glaze and serve hot with low-fat plain yogurt or fat-free fromage frais.

INGREDIENTS

1 pineapple	2.5-cm/1-inch piece of fresh
1 papaya	root ginger, grated
1 mango	4 kiwi fruit, peeled and sliced
6 tbsp clear honey	2 nectarines, peeled, stoned
grated rind of 1 orange	and halved
grated rind of 1 lemon	2 bananas, peeled and halved

NUTRITIONAL INFORMATION

Calories 320

Protein 4g

Carbohydrate 79g

Sugars 78g

Fat 1g

Saturates 0g

variation

Other fruits that are delicious cooked in the same way include peaches, apples and pears. They all cook equally well on a barbecue.

cook's tip

Use a single flower honey, if possible. Try clover, acacia, orange blossom or lavender – they will impart a delicious flavour to the grilled fruit.

1 Preheat the grill to medium. Using a sharp knife, cut the plume off the pineapple and discard. Stand the pineapple upright and slice off the skin. Remove any eyes and slice into rings. Set 4 rings aside and store the rest in the refrigerator for another day.

2 Cut the papaya in half and scoop out the seeds with a metal spoon. Peel and slice. Set aside 4 slices and store the rest in the refrigerator for another day.

3 Slice the mango in half through to the stone, then twist to remove the flesh from the stone. Peel and slice the flesh, set 4 slices aside and store the rest in the refrigerator for another day.

4 Mix the honey, orange and lemon rind and ginger together in a bowl. Place the reserved pineapple, papaya and mango on a grill rack with the kiwi fruit, nectarines and bananas. Brush the honey glaze over the fruit.

5 Cook the fruit under the preheated grill for 10 minutes, brushing with the glaze and turning frequently. Divide between 4 serving plates and serve immediately.

fig & watermelon salad

serves 4 **prep: 15 mins,** ⟳ **plus 1 hr chilling** **cook: 5 mins** ⟳

Fruit salads are always popular, and are quick and easy to prepare. Ring the changes with this attractive summery combination that looks almost too pretty to eat.

INGREDIENTS

1 watermelon, weighing
about 1.5 kg/3 lb 5 oz

115 g/4 oz seedless black grapes

4 figs

1 lime

grated rind and juice of 1 orange

1 tbsp maple syrup

2 tbsp clear honey

4 fresh mint sprigs, to decorate

(optional)

NUTRITIONAL INFORMATION

Calories 169

Protein 2g

Carbohydrate 41g

Sugars 40g

Fat 1g

Saturates 0g

variation

Add 2 pieces of finely chopped stem ginger to the fruit in Step 1 and substitute 1 tablespoon of ginger syrup from the jar for the maple syrup.

1 Cut the watermelon into quarters and scoop out and discard the seeds. Cut the flesh away from the rind, then chop the flesh into 2.5-cm/1-inch cubes. Place the watermelon cubes in a bowl with the grapes. Cut each fig lengthways into 8 wedges and add to the bowl.

2 Grate the lime rind and mix it with the orange rind and juice, maple syrup and honey in a small saucepan. Bring to the boil over a low heat. Pour the mixture over the fruit and stir. Leave to cool. Stir again, cover and chill in the refrigerator for at least 1 hour, stirring occasionally.

3 To serve, divide the fruit salad equally between 4 glass dishes and decorate with a fresh mint sprig, if you like.

stuffed baked apples

🍳 **cook: 45 mins**   🕐 **prep: 10 mins**   **serves 4**

Baked apples are a traditional family favourite, and are often stuffed with sultanas, raisins and brown sugar. Try this ginger-flavoured flapjack stuffing for a change.

NUTRITIONAL INFORMATION	
Calories	170
Protein	3g
Carbohydrate	31g
Sugars	23g
Fat	5g
Saturates	0g

INGREDIENTS

25 g/1 oz blanched almonds

55 g/2 oz no-soak dried apricots

1 piece stem ginger, drained

1 tbsp clear honey

1 tbsp syrup from the stem ginger jar

4 tbsp rolled oats

4 large cooking apples

1 Preheat the oven to 180°C/350°F/Gas Mark 4. Using a sharp knife, chop the almonds very finely. Chop the apricots and stem ginger very finely. Set aside.

2 Put the honey and syrup in a saucepan and heat until the honey has melted. Stir in the oats and cook gently over a low heat

for 2 minutes. Remove the saucepan from the heat and stir in the almonds, apricots, and stem ginger.

3 Core the apples, widen the tops slightly and score around the circumference of each to prevent the skins from bursting during cooking. Place them in an ovenproof dish and fill the cavities with

the stuffing. Pour just enough water into the dish to come about one-third of the way up the apples. Bake in the oven for 40 minutes, or until tender. Serve immediately.

hot chocolate cherries

serves 4   **prep: 15 mins**   **cook: 25 mins**

*This is a naughty self-indulgence, but chocoholics don't have to
forego their favourite fix and there is even double cream in this
melt-in-the-mouth dessert. It makes a good finale to a dinner party.*

INGREDIENTS

4 tbsp water

55 g/2 oz caster sugar

1 strip of pared lemon rind

450 g/1 lb sweet black cherries, stoned

1 tbsp cocoa powder

pinch of salt

4 tbsp double cream

4 tbsp maraschino liqueur
or cherry brandy

NUTRITIONAL INFORMATION

Calories 280

Protein 2g

Carbohydrate 31g

Sugars 31g

Fat 15g

Saturates 9g

variation

Instead of lemon rind, flavour the
syrup with a vanilla pod and remove it
in Step 2, or add ½ teaspoon vanilla
extract with the liqueur in Step 3.

cook's tip

Don't substitute single cream
for the double cream – even
with the intention of lowering
the fat content of this recipe –
because it will curdle.

1 Preheat the grill to medium. Put the water, sugar and lemon rind in a saucepan and bring to the boil over a low heat, stirring constantly, until the sugar has dissolved. Add the cherries and cook, stirring, for 1 minute. Remove from the heat. Using a slotted spoon, transfer the cherries to a flameproof dish. Reserve the syrup.

2 Put the cocoa powder in a bowl and mix in the salt. Whisking constantly, pour in the cream in a steady stream. Remove the lemon rind from the syrup and discard, then stir in the cream mixture. Return to the heat and bring to the boil, stirring. Simmer the mixture over a low heat for 10–15 minutes, or until reduced by about half.

3 Remove from the heat, and stir in the maraschino liqueur. Pour the sauce over the cherries. Cook under the preheated grill for 2 minutes, then serve.

banana soufflés

serves 4   **prep: 10 mins**   **cook: 8 mins**

These elegant individual soufflés would be an excellent choice for a special dinner party dessert, especially as they are so simple to make. Like all soufflés, however, they must be served immediately otherwise they will begin to deflate.

INGREDIENTS

3 large, ripe peaches   1 tsp Southern Comfort or

1 tbsp lemon juice   peach schnapps

1 tbsp clear honey   peach leaves, to decorate

NUTRITIONAL INFORMATION

Calories 194

Protein 7g

Carbohydrate 27g

Sugars 26g

Fat 7g

Saturates 2g

variation

Replace the Malibu with ordinary rum or orange juice and substitute lemon juice for the lime juice.

cook's tip

To whisk egg whites well, make sure that they are as fresh as possible and that they are at room temperature. Use a clean, dry, grease-free bowl and a balloon whisk or electric beaters.

1 Preheat the oven to 230°C/450°F/Gas Mark 8. Lightly brush 4 x 350-ml/ 12-fl-oz soufflé dishes with oil. Peel the bananas and cut into 2.5-cm/1-inch lengths, then place in a food processor with the lime juice and liqueur. Process until smooth. Add the egg yolks and 1 teaspoon of the sugar and process briefly again. Transfer to a bowl.

2 Place the egg whites in a spotlessly clean, greasefree bowl and whisk until stiff peaks form, then whisk in the remaining sugar, 1 tablespoon at a time, until the mixture becomes stiff and glossy. Fold 1 tablespoon of the egg white mixture into the banana mixture to loosen it, then gently incorporate the remainder.

3 Spoon the soufflé mixture into the prepared dishes and make a rim with the end of a teaspoon. Place on a baking sheet and bake in the oven for 8 minutes, or until well risen and golden. Dust with icing sugar and serve immediately.

nectarine crunch

serves 3   **prep: 10 mins**   **cook: 0 mins**

This incredibly easy and nutritious dessert is very popular with children, who even enjoy making it themselves. You can vary the fruit, fruit nectar and jam according to the season.

INGREDIENTS

4 nectarines

175 g/6 oz raisin and nut crunchy oat cereal

300 ml/10 fl oz low-fat natural yogurt

2 tbsp peach jam

2 tbsp peach nectar

NUTRITIONAL INFORMATION	
Calories	.419
Protein	.15g
Carbohydrate	.83g
Sugars	.52g
Fat	.5g
Saturates	.0g

cook's tip

There is no need to peel the nectarines – just wash and pat dry with kitchen paper. If you use peaches, they work better if they are peeled.

1 Using a sharp knife, cut the nectarines in half, then remove and discard the stones. Chop the flesh into bite-sized pieces. Reserve a few pieces for decoration and place a few pieces in the bottom of 3 sundae glasses.

Place a layer of oat cereal in each glass, then drizzle over a little yogurt.

2 Place the jam and peach nectar in a large jug and stir together to mix. Add a few more nectarine

pieces to the glasses and drizzle over a little of the jam mixture. Continue building up the layers in this way, finishing with a layer of yogurt and a sprinkling of oat cereal. Decorate with the reserved nectarine pieces and serve.

lemon brûlées with redcurrants

⏱ **cook: 10 mins**

⏲ **prep: 10 mins, plus 30 mins chilling**

serves 4

Concealed beneath the caramelised topping is a surprising fruity sauce. Made with yogurt rather than cream, these little desserts are wonderful low-fat treats which are perfect for any occasion.

NUTRITIONAL INFORMATION

Calories	.250
Protein	.10g
Carbohydrate	.23g
Sugars	.23g
Fat	.14g
Saturates	.8g

INGREDIENTS

1 lemon

175 g/6 oz redcurrants, plus extra
to decorate

3 tbsp caster sugar

600 ml/1 pint Greek yogurt

¼ tsp ground cinnamon

variation

These brûlées are equally delicious made with other berries such as blackcurrants, whitecurrants, billberries or blueberries.

1 Grate the rind from the lemon and set aside. Preheat the grill to medium. Put the redcurrants and 1 tablespoon of the sugar in a small, heavy-based saucepan and cook over a low heat until the juices begin to run. Remove from the heat, stir in the lemon rind and set aside.

2 Mix the yogurt and ground cinnamon together in a bowl. Divide the redcurrants between 4 ramekin dishes or small flameproof dishes. Top with the cinnamon yogurt and sprinkle with the remaining sugar. Place under the preheated grill for 4–5 minutes, or until the sugar is golden brown and bubbling.

Cool and leave to chill in the refrigerator for at least 30 minutes before serving. When ready to serve, decorate with the extra redcurrants.

berry yogurt ice

serves 4   **prep: 15 mins,**   **cook: 5 mins**
plus 4 hrs freezing

This refreshing ice makes a wonderful summer dessert after a filling meal, as it is light and cooling without the richness – or fat – of ice cream. Serve with a selection of fresh summer berries.

INGREDIENTS

125 g/4½ oz raspberries	175 ml/6 fl oz Greek yogurt
125 g/4½ oz blackberries	125 ml/4 fl oz red wine
125 g/4½ oz strawberries	2¼ tsp powdered gelatine
1 large egg	fresh berries, to decorate

NUTRITIONAL INFORMATION

Calories 118

Protein 6g

Carbohydrate 6g

Sugars 6g

Fat 6g

Saturates 3g

variation

Substitute 55 g/2 oz redcurrants for half the raspberries and 55 g/2 oz blackcurrants for half the blackberries.

cook's tip

Vegetarians can use a vegetarian gelatine, which is available in health food shops, to make this ice. Follow the instructions on the packet and proceed as in main recipe.

 Put the raspberries, blackberries and strawberries in a blender or food processor and process until a smooth purée forms. Rub the purée through a sieve into a bowl to remove the seeds.

2 Break the egg and separate the yolk and white into separate bowls. Stir

the egg yolk and yogurt into the berry purée and set the egg white aside.

3 Pour the wine into a heatproof bowl and sprinkle the gelatine on the surface. Leave to stand for 5 minutes to soften, then set the bowl over a saucepan of simmering water until the gelatine has dissolved. Pour

the mixture into the berry purée in a steady stream, whisking constantly. Transfer the mixture to a freezerproof container and freeze for 2 hours, or until slushy.

4 Whisk the egg white in a spotlessly clean, greasefree bowl until very stiff. Remove the berry mixture from the freezer and fold in

the egg white. Return to the freezer and freeze for 2 hours, or until firm. To serve, scoop the berry yogurt ice into glass dishes and decorate with fresh berries of your choice.

coffee ice cream

serves 6

prep: 1 hr, plus 6 hrs freezing

cook: 0 mins

This Italian-style dessert tastes as if it is full of double cream. In fact, it isn't an ice cream at all. If you have an espresso machine, make the coffee in that, otherwise brew it double strength in a filter.

INGREDIENTS

25 g/1 oz plain chocolate

225 g/8 oz ricotta cheese

5 tbsp low-fat natural yogurt

85 g/3 oz caster sugar

175 ml/6 fl oz strong black coffee, cooled and chilled

½ tsp ground cinnamon

dash of vanilla essence

25 g/1 oz chocolate curls, to decorate

NUTRITIONAL INFORMATION	
Calories	150
Protein	6g
Carbohydrate	21g
Sugars	21g
Fat	6g
Saturates	4g

variation

Omit the cinnamon and vanilla essence and substitute 40 g/1½ oz grated mint chocolate for the plain chocolate.

1 Grate the chocolate and set aside. Put the ricotta cheese, yogurt and sugar in a blender or food processor and process until a smooth purée forms. Transfer to a large bowl and beat in the coffee, cinnamon, vanilla essence and grated chocolate.

2 Spoon the mixture into a freezerproof container

and freeze for 1½ hours, or until slushy. Remove from the freezer, turn into a bowl and beat. Return to the container and freeze for 1½ hours.

3 Repeat this beating and freezing process twice more before serving in scoops, decorated with chocolate curls. Alternatively, leave in the freezer until 15 minutes before

serving, then transfer to the refrigerator to soften slightly before scooping.

lemon granita

cook: 5 mins

prep: 10 mins, plus 2 hrs freezing

serves 4

Not quite a sorbet, but more than a cold drink, a granita is a deliciously refreshing way to cleanse the palate, and is an ideal dessert to serve after a spicy main course.

NUTRITIONAL INFORMATION	
Calories	115
Protein	0g
Carbohydrate	31g
Sugars	31g
Fat	0g
Saturates	0g

INGREDIENTS

450 ml/16 fl oz water

115 g/4 oz sugar

grated rind of 1 lemon

8 tbsp freshly squeezed lemon juice

lemon zest, to decorate

1 Put the water and sugar in a large, heavy-based saucepan and set over a low heat. Stir until the sugar has completely dissolved. Bring to the boil, then remove the saucepan from the heat and leave to cool.

2 Add the lemon rind and juice to the cooled syrup and stir well to combine, then pour the mixture into a large, shallow, freezerproof container and freeze for 2 hours, or until the lemon syrup is solid.

3 Plunge the base of the container into hot water for 30 seconds, then turn out the frozen syrup into a food processor. Process to small crystals, then spoon into serving bowls and decorate with lemon zest. Serve immediately.

variation

You can substitute the grated rind of ½ orange and the same quantity of orange juice for the lemon rind and juice, if you like.

peach sorbet

serves 4   **prep: 10 mins,** ⟳ **plus 2 hrs freezing**   **cook: 0 mins** ⟳

This is a cheating, but still effective way of making a luscious frozen dessert, full of intense fruit flavour. Serve in small dessert bowls as part of a dinner party menu.

INGREDIENTS

3 large, ripe peaches

1 tbsp lemon juice

1 tbsp clear honey

1 tsp Southern Comfort or peach schnapps

peach leaves, to decorate

NUTRITIONAL INFORMATION	
Calories	.57
Protein	.1g
Carbohydrate	.13g
Sugars	.13g
Fat	.0g
Saturates	.0g

variation

For a virtually instant strawberry sorbet, buy 500 g/1 lb 2 oz frozen strawberries and process as in main recipe with honey and Curaço.

cook's tip

To peel a whole peach, make a tiny nick in the skin and place in a bowl. Cover with boiling water and leave for 15 seconds. Remove using a slotted spoon. Peel off the skin.

1 Using a sharp knife, cut the peaches in half, then remove and discard the stones. Place the peach halves in a bowl of boiling water and leave for 15 seconds. Remove from the bowl using a slotted spoon and peel off the skins. Cut the peaches into 2.5-cm/1-inch chunks and toss with the lemon juice. Spread the chunks out on a baking sheet, cover with clingfilm and freeze for 2 hours, or until solid.

2 Remove the peaches from the freezer and place in a food processor. Pulse until granular, scraping down the sides from time to time.

3 Add the honey and Southern Comfort and process again until thoroughly blended and fairly firm in consistency. Serve immediately, decorated with peach leaves or place in a freezerproof container and store in the freezer for up to 24 hours.

indonesian black rice pudding

serves 4   **prep: 5 mins** 🕒   **cook: 45 mins** 🕒

Also known as glutinous rice, even though it doesn't contain any gluten, sticky rice is available from Chinese supermarkets and may be black or white – the former is unpolished.

INGREDIENTS

115 g/4 oz black sticky rice

450 ml/16 fl oz water

55 g/2 oz dark brown sugar

55 g/2 oz caster sugar

300 ml/10 fl oz coconut milk, to serve

NUTRITIONAL INFORMATION

Calories 228

Protein 3g

Carbohydrate 54g

Sugars 33g

Fat 1g

Saturates 0g

variation

Add a small piece of bruised fresh root ginger when cooking the rice to add extra flavour. Remove and discard before serving.

1 Rinse the black sticky rice under cold running water, drain and place in a large, heavy-based saucepan. Add the water and bring to the boil, stirring constantly. Cover and simmer over a medium–low heat for 30 minutes.

2 Stir in the two sugars and cook for a further 15 minutes. If necessary, add a little more water to prevent the rice from sticking.

3 Ladle the rice into 4 warmed bowls and serve immediately with the coconut milk. Alternatively, leave to cool completely and serve cold.

magic cheesecake

cook: 5 mins

prep: 15 mins, plus 1 hr chilling

serves 6

This superb dessert proves that you can have your cake and eat it too – or rather, you can indulge in a wonderful creamy and luxurious cheesecake and still stick to a healthy low-fat diet.

NUTRITIONAL INFORMATION

Calories	175
Protein	9g
Carbohydrate	22g
Sugars	12g
Fat	6g
Saturates	2g

INGREDIENTS

350 g/12 oz mixed fruits, such as star fruit, kiwi fruit, strawberries and kumquats

115 g/4 oz bran flakes, crushed

55 g/2 oz low-fat spread

280 g/10 oz firm tofu (drained weight)

200 ml/7 fl oz low-fat natural yogurt

1 tbsp powdered gelatine

6 tbsp apple juice

variation

If you like, try adding some finely grated lemon rind and the juice of 1 lemon to the yogurt and tofu mixture for extra flavour.

1 Prepare the fruits to lay on top of the cheesecake by washing, deseeding, peeling and slicing, as necessary, and set aside. Place the bran flakes in a polythene bag and crush them with a rolling pin.

2 Place the low-fat spread and 2 tablespoons of the apple juice in a saucepan

over a very low heat and stir. When the spread has melted, stir in the bran flakes. Turn the mixture into a 23-cm/9-inch loose-based cake tin and press down with a wooden spoon to cover the base. Set aside.

3 Put the tofu and yogurt in a food processor and process until smooth, then transfer to a bowl. Pour the

remaining apple juice into a heatproof bowl, sprinkle the gelatine over the surface and leave to stand for 5 minutes to soften. Set the bowl over a saucepan of simmering water for 5 minutes, or until the gelatine has dissolved, then pour into the tofu mixture in a steady stream, beating constantly. Spread over the base and chill until set.

4 Remove the cheesecake from the tin and place on a serving plate. Arrange the mixed fruits on top and serve.

fat-free marble cake

serves 8   **prep: 25 mins**   **cook: 45 mins**

For those of us who have a particularly sweet tooth, this beautifully light cake is too good to be true. The secret of its success lies in sifting the flour several times.

INGREDIENTS

sunflower oil, for brushing

100 g/3½ oz plain flour, sifted, plus extra for dusting

3 tbsp cocoa powder

225 g/8 oz caster sugar

pinch of salt

10 egg whites

1 tsp cream of tartar

½ tsp almond essence

½ tsp vanilla essence

icing sugar, for dusting

NUTRITIONAL INFORMATION

Calories 186

Protein 6g

Carbohydrate 40g

Sugars 30g

Fat 1g

Saturates 1g

cook's tip

When removing the baked cake from the oven, leave inverted in the tin on a wire rack, then tap the base gently all the way round. This will release it from the tin.

1 Preheat the oven to 180°C/350°F/Gas Mark 4. Oil and dust a 20-cm/8-inch deep cake tin. Sift 40 g/1½ oz of the flour with the cocoa powder and 2 tablespoons of the sugar into a bowl 4 times. Sift the remaining flour with 2 tablespoons of the sugar and the salt into a separate bowl 4 times.

2 Beat the egg whites in a spotlessly clean, grease-free bowl until soft peaks form. Add the cream of tartar and beat in the remaining caster sugar, 1 tablespoonful at a time, until the egg whites form stiff peaks. Whisk in the almond and vanilla essences. Divide the mixture in half. Fold the cocoa and flour mixture into one half and the unflavoured flour into the other half. Spoon the cocoa flavoured mixture into the tin and top with the unflavoured mixture. Run a round-bladed knife through both mixtures to create a marbled effect.

3 Bake in the preheated oven for 45 minutes, or until a skewer inserted into the centre of the cake comes out clean. Invert onto a wire rack to cool and dust with icing sugar before serving.

citrus honey cake

cook: 35 mins   **prep: 20 mins**   serves 8

This light-textured cake is drizzled with honey and lemon juice while it is still warm from the oven, giving it a rich and zesty flavour. Serve as a delicious dessert or a tasty afternoon snack.

NUTRITIONAL INFORMATION	
Calories	158
Protein	4g
Carbohydrate	30g
Sugars	11g
Fat	3g
Saturates	1g

INGREDIENTS

sunflower or corn oil, for brushing

40 g/1½ oz reduced-fat sunflower margarine

4 tbsp clear honey

finely grated rind and juice of 1 lemon

150 ml/5 fl oz skimmed milk

140 g/5 oz plain flour

1½ tsp baking powder

½ teaspoon mixed spice

55 g/2 oz semolina

2 egg whites

2 tsp sesame seeds

cook's tip

Greek Hymettus honey, which has a distinctive aroma of thyme, would be especially delicious in this cake, as would the less expensive lemon blossom honey.

1 Preheat the oven to 200°C/400°F/Gas Mark 6. Lightly brush a 23-cm/9-inch round cake tin with oil and line the base with baking paper. Put the margarine and 3 tablespoons of the honey in a heavy-based saucepan and melt over a very low heat. Remove from the heat. Reserve 1 tablespoon of the lemon juice and stir the remainder into the honey mixture with the lemon rind and milk.

2 Sift the flour, baking powder and mixed spice into a bowl, then beat the mixture into the saucepan. Beat in the semolina. Whisk the egg whites in a separate spotlessly clean, greasefree bowl until soft peaks form, then gently fold them into the mixture. Spoon into the prepared tin and smooth the surface. Sprinkle the sesame seeds evenly on top.

3 Bake the cake in the preheated oven for 30 minutes, or until golden brown and springy to the touch. Mix the remaining honey and lemon juice in a small jug and pour it over the cake. Leave in the tin to cool before serving.

apricot cake

serves 8

prep: 20 mins, plus 40 mins cooling and chilling ⏲

cook: 1 hr 15 mins ⏲

The moist, fruity layer of filling makes this lovely light cake a welcome treat with a cup of mid-morning coffee or as a dessert at the end of a midweek family supper.

INGREDIENTS

BASE

200 g/7 oz plain flour, plus extra for dusting

pinch of salt

55 g/2 oz caster sugar

grated rind of ½ lemon

4 tbsp water

90 g/3¼ oz unsalted butter, softened

FILLING

125 g/4½ oz short-grain rice

450 ml/16 fl oz skimmed milk

85 g/3 oz caster sugar

grated rind and juice of ½ lemon

1 tbsp apricot jam

3 eggs, separated

800 g/1 lb 12 oz apricots, peeled, halved and stoned

icing sugar, for dusting

NUTRITIONAL INFORMATION

Calories 377

Protein 9g

Carbohydrate 63g

Sugars 24g

Fat 12g

Saturates 7g

variation

For a change, replace the grated lemon rind and juice in the base and filling with the same amount of grated orange rind and juice.

cook's tip

To bake blind, prick the base all over with a fork, then line with baking paper. Partially fill with baking beans – either ceramic beans, or dried haricot beans kept specially for the purpose – and bake.

1 Preheat the oven to 200°C/400°F/Gas Mark 6. Sift the flour with a pinch of salt into a bowl and add the sugar, lemon rind, water and butter. Mix well, using an electric mixer or fork, until crumbly. Turn out onto a lightly floured work surface and knead lightly until smooth. Roll out and use to line the base and 3-cm/1¼-inches of the sides of a 25-cm/10-inch springform cake tin. Chill in the refrigerator for 30 minutes, then bake blind in the oven for 10 minutes (see Cook's Tip).

2 Meanwhile, make the filling. Put the rice, milk, sugar and lemon rind in a small, heavy-based saucepan and bring to the boil. Reduce the heat and simmer for 30 minutes. Remove the saucepan from the heat, stir in the lemon juice and apricot jam and leave to cool.

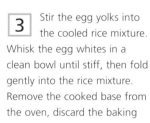

3 Stir the egg yolks into the cooled rice mixture. Whisk the egg whites in a clean bowl until stiff, then fold gently into the rice mixture. Remove the cooked base from the oven, discard the baking beans and lining paper and reduce the oven temperature to 180°C/350°F/Gas Mark 4. Arrange the apricot halves, flat side uppermost, over the base. Spoon the rice mixture over the top, spreading it out evenly. Bake for 45 minutes, or until a skewer inserted into the cake comes out clean. Cool on a wire rack and dust with icing sugar before serving.

makes about 40   **prep: 30 mins**   **cook: 30 mins**

Traditionally, these moreish little Italian macaroons are made with apricot kernels, but almonds are used here. Serve amaretti with iced desserts or coffee at the end of a dinner party.

INGREDIENTS

150 g/5½ oz blanched almonds

150 g/5½ oz caster sugar

1 large egg white

icing sugar, for dusting

NUTRITIONAL INFORMATION

Calories 38

Protein 1g

Carbohydrate 4g

Sugars 4g

Fat 2g

Saturates 0g

 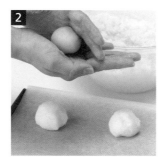 

cook's tip

Commercially cooked amaretti obtain their distinctive flavour from a judicious mix of sweet and bitter almonds. Bitter almonds are not available to the home cook as they have to be washed with extreme care.

1 Preheat the oven to 120°C/250°F/Gas Mark ½. Put the almonds and caster sugar in a mortar and crush with a pestle. Alternatively, finely chop the almonds and then mix with the sugar in a bowl.

2 Lightly beat the egg white, then stir it into the almond mixture to form a firm dough. Pull away walnut-sized pieces of dough and roll between your palms into small balls. Line 2 baking sheets with baking paper and place the dough pieces on them, spaced well apart. Dust with icing sugar. Bake in the preheated oven for 30 minutes, then transfer to wire racks to cool completely. Serve.

fruity flapjacks

⏱ **cook: 15–20 mins** ⏱ **prep: 10 mins** **makes 14**

Great favourites with children for after-school snacks, and extremely popular with mums, too, these tasty cereal bars are healthy, inexpensive and incredibly easy to make.

NUTRITIONAL INFORMATION	
Calories	120
Protein	2g
Carbohydrate	19g
Sugars	13g
Fat	5g
Saturates	1g

INGREDIENTS

sunflower or corn oil, for brushing

140 g/5 oz rolled oats

115 g/4 oz demerara sugar

85 g/3 oz raisins

115 g/4 oz low-fat sunflower
margarine, melted

variation

You can substitute the same quantity of dried cranberries or blueberries for the raisins. These are now available in most large supermarkets.

1 Preheat the oven to 190°C/375°F/Gas Mark 5. Lightly brush a 28 x 18 cm/11 x 7-inch shallow rectangular cake tin with oil.

2 Mix the oats, sugar, raisins and margarine together in a bowl and stir.

3 Spoon the oat mixture into the prepared tin and press down firmly with the back of a spoon. Bake in the oven for 15–20 minutes, or until golden brown.

4 Using a sharp knife, score lines to mark out 14 bars, then leave to cool in the tin for 10 minutes. Transfer the bars to a wire rack to cool completely.

index

index